Old Cottage and Domestic Architecture in South-West Surrey, and Notes On the Early History of the Division

Ralph Nevill

OLD COTTAGE

AND

DOMESTIC ARCHITECTURE

IN

SOUTH - WEST SURREY,

AND

Notes on the Early History of the Division.

BY

RALPH NEVILL, F.S.A., F.R.I.B.A.

GUILDFORD:

PRINTED BY BILLING & SONS.

1889.

CONTENTS.

PART I.

ARCHITECTURAL.

PART II.

TOPOGRAPHICAL AND PLATES.

PART III.

ROMAN AND OTHER EARLY SETTLEMENTS IN SOUTH-WEST SURREY.

PREFACE.

SOME sixteen years ago I published some sketches of old Surrey cottages in the 'Spring Gardens Sketch-book,' a private work connected with the office of the late Sir G. G. Scott. Since then material has accumulated, and has led to this attempt to treat the subject.

I have said elsewhere, that the sketches are intended, above all things, to show the architecture, and I will only ask further, that they be not judged by the standard of etchings, woodcuts, or the other similar processes now in use. The drawings were originally published in the *Builder*, and the process of lithography employed for the purpose has its limits. I have regarded it as of the first importance to make the sketches as absolutely faithful as possible. I have not, therefore, added anything for effect; on the other hand, it is fair to say that the buildings cannot always be seen exactly as I show them, since in many cases it has been necessary to omit trees, the angles of haystacks, or sheds that impeded any possible view. I have also frequently omitted gutters and down-spouts; these are always modern, and generally recklessly fixed, and could not be shown on so small a scale without seriously inter-fering with the intelligibility of the drawings. I have, however, shown them on town houses, or places where they were part of the design.

I had originally intended a much more thorough historical treatment of cottage building; I found, however, that to be of any use, this would take time and labour that could not now be given to it. In especial, I had wished to incorporate notices from surveys of manors, old wills, and other such sources bearing on the plans of cottages and houses.

I have relinquished this, for the present, the more readily that it will be of much more value when a greater amount of information, such as I have here endeavoured to put together, has been accumulated. This is particularly the case with plans not only of cottages, but of the humbler class of house. Parker's well-known book on 'Domestic Architecture' deals efficiently with the more important mansions, but I do not know of any collection of such plans as I have given. I am myself now publishing in the *Builder* a similar series of papers on stone cottages, etc., near Stroud, in Gloucestershire, and I venture to hope that many other parts of our country will eventually be illustrated in the same way; any attempt at a history of the subject had therefore better be postponed for the present.

In Part II. I have endeavoured to give some topographical information, and in especial to record such facts as are not to be found in the county histories by Manning and Bray, or Brayley.

I am inclined to apologize for the length of Part III. I had originally intended to put into a short chapter such matter as would be of interest to those living in the neighbourhood; as I went on, this expanded into the present part. I hope it will at least prove of local interest, and I must ask others to look on it as an extra thrown in, as, indeed, it has only come into existence since the arrangements for publication were completed.

Since this matter was put into type, I find that Mr. Elton, in his 'Origins of English History,' made, years ago, nearly the same remarks as I have, as to the civilization of the South Saxons; I make the explanation lest I should be thought guilty of borrowing without acknowledgment.

I have often referred to Mr. H. F. Napper; besides personal correspondence, papers by this gentleman will be found in 'Sussex Archæological Transactions,' vol. xxxiv., and, within the last week, in 'Surrey Archæological Transactions,' vol. ix., part ii. I by no means pledge myself to an acceptance of his conclusions, but refer to them as of value as the observations of one well acquainted with the localities and enjoying the immense advantages of the Ordnance Survey; both of these were wanting to those who first wrote on the subject and whose opinions seem to have been repeated ever since without any serious attempt at local investigation.

In conclusion, I will express a hope that leniency will be shown to the faults that must inevitably attend the first attempt to deal systematically with any subject. The subject itself will, I trust, prove attractive not only to those interested in the art of architecture, but to all students of one of the most important periods of our history, and to those Transatlantic cousins who may claim an equal interest in the homes where our forefathers dwelt.

RALPH NEVILL,

Rolls Chambers, Chancery Lane.

July 1, 1889.

NOTE.—I am sorry I was not in time to withdraw a suggested derivation on page 117, which on reflection I feel is probably 'groundless.' Nothing is more dangerous than guesses at etymology, and with this exception I have attempted nothing in this way except to give references to actual documents.

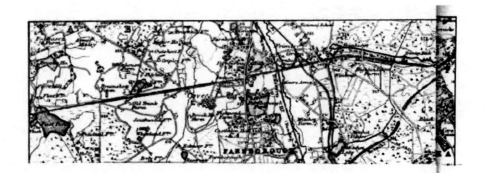

INDEX TO ILLUSTRATIONS.

PLATES.

TEXT-CUTS.

OLD COTTAGE AND DOMESTIC ARCHITECTURE.

SURREY: SOUTH-WEST.

CHAPTER I.

INTRODUCTORY.

THOUGH our old cottages have long been favourite subjects for painters and though they have evidently been studied by many of our architects, I do not know of any attempt at systematic illustration of them from an architectural point of view. That such illustration is most desirable will readily be conceded, in view of the rapid manner in which natural decay and modern improvements are sweeping away the genuine examples.

I have not confined myself entirely to cottages, but have included other domestic buildings of the same character, omitting only those of more strictly architectural design and important nature. My principal object being architectural, my subjects are chosen from that, rather than from a picturesque point of view and my aim has been to give an intelligible rendering of the architecture, to the exclusion of the accidents of light, shade and colour that actually add so much to the beauty of the subjects. I have endeavoured, therefore, not so much to produce pictures as illustrations that can be exactly understood in all their details.

I must say that many of my sketches were made as long as twenty years ago and that in revisiting the places I have, in several instances, found changes. I have kept the old forms as of more interest than the new.

In what I am writing I make no pretence to give a complete history either of cottages or of the style of any period. On the contrary, I aim only at contributing such notes of one district as it is necessary to have of all, before we can generalize.

I have endeavoured to show how to make the study of our humbler ancient buildings valuable architecturally, but I have tried not to intrude any special fancies of my own, but to put into words the accepted ideas of those of us who have studied and worked at the style, for the benefit of others who have perhaps not had the time nor the opportunity of so doing, and yet may be anxious for knowledge. Much of what I say on the architectural features will doubtless appear very elementary, but it is only too true that even such elementary knowledge is sadly wanted.

Moreover, one constantly sees examples where a certain outward appearance of style has been achieved, but united to gross faults of taste and knowledge, arising from ignorance of these little elementary facts.

Many of the examples best known to painters will not be found here, nor some of those interesting to archæologists ; but as I may claim to have inspected nearly every example, new or old, in the district selected, I believe I may say that I have hardly omitted anything which seemed to have a useful lesson to convey.

The great lesson to be learned from the study of these old examples is, I take it, the extreme value of simplicity. It is a lesson peculiarly needed, since even when an architect is anxious to work on such lines, it is seldom that his client is content to let him.

There is far more beauty in a cottage of some of the simpler forms shown, with its roof bright with lichen and its front covered with creepers, than we shall ever get from modern examples, tortured as they are into fantastic shapes where all repose and simplicity are lost.

Anxious, however, as the landowner generally is, to secure economy of cost, it is not often that he can be persuaded to trust to simplicity of line and good proportion rather than to overcrowded gables and fantastic bargeboards.

On the other hand, I do not wish to be taken as suggesting that any plain building will look well. On the contrary, well thought out and planned proportion is, as in all architecture, of the greatest importance and much is to be gained by the inclusion of some of the many features illustrated in my drawings, as long as the mistake is not made of crowding them all into one building.

I have been told that some of my examples are not 'architecture' at all, but 'barns.' It is precisely the importance of perfectly simple treatment of simple buildings, that I want to enforce by the exhibition of old examples, the picturesqueness of which, as compared with modern efforts, is universally admitted.

The bounds of my district are those of the present Parliamentary Division of Guildford, or South-west Surrey. This is, roughly speaking, a square taken out of the south-west corner of Surrey.

I have, on consideration, chosen this very modern division, because it is more convenient, and represents facts of settlement and inhabitation better than the more ancient division of Hundreds. These latter were doubtless convenient at the time they were made, but have had none but a legal bearing on the later history with which I am dealing.

In two cases, the examples at Abinger Hatch and Paddington Manor, I unwittingly went over the border, but there is the excuse that, by connection, both these places belong to this division rather than to the Dorking district.

I have purposely confined myself to narrow limits, since it has always seemed to me best to choose a certain district and illustrate that completely, rather than to roam about picking out the architectural plums and neglecting the small details, the study of which is quite as important.

If a particular district be taken, or a particular subject be studied, or illustrated, exhaustively, the work remains on record for ever, whereas hundreds of clever but desultory sketches are perpetually being published and forgotten for lack of some point of attachment.

My own feeling is that an architectural student will do best for himself by making a thorough and systematic study of his own neighbourhood, with its three or four centuries of good work, before he begins to rove the country in search of novelties.

I would urge the importance of this home study, especially on local schools of Art, who might do the most useful work by directing to it the energies of their students.

The art of building, to be really living and successful among us, must not depend on the efforts of a few architects, but must be the possession of the whole of those concerned in the building trades. The builder, his clerk and his workmen, may, by a diligent study of the good old work that exists all round them, improve themselves just as architects have, since they took to more diligent study. They may then pick up again the tradition rudely interrupted at the beginning of the century, and they will certainly add a new interest and pleasure to their lives, and spare the public the purposeless and wanton atrocities that so disfigure our land.

There is more real advantage to be gained from a diligent and discriminating study of actual buildings than by the assimilation of any number of text-books, valuable as they may be. The more intimately the student is acquainted with old work, the less eager will he be to parade his insufficient powers under the specious but terrible plea of being original.

I have found it impossible so to arrange this book that the illustrations shall coincide altogether with the letterpress they illustrate, since in that case architectural and topographical matter would be inextricably mixed up. I propose, therefore, to go first, seriatim, through the architectural features and afterwards to go through the sketches topographically. It will be perhaps inevitable that I shall repeat myself somewhat and I must therefore ask the indulgence of the reader for that which will be done in the hope of saving him trouble.

CHAPTER II.

DATE AND STYLE.

THE date of the greater part of the cottages in this district is sixteenth century and especially its latter half and the first half of the seventeenth century.

In the Domesday Survey, I find that, leaving out Guildford where there were 175 homines and sundry others, there were in the division 376 villani, 183 bordarii and cotarii (the term is used indifferently) and 39 servi, or slaves.

In the various surveys of manors constant mention is made of cottages.

In the grant * purporting to be from Burghred, King of Mercia to Croyland Abbey, in A.D. 868, Spalding is said to have 24 mansiones and 80 cotagia; Deping, 200 mansiones and 400 cotagia; and Kirkby, 1 mansio and 3 cotagia. This charter is, no doubt, a medieval forgery, but may be taken as evidence of what existed at the time of its forgery.

I shall, perhaps, be asked what has become of these older cottages, since I limit the date of those that remain to the sixteenth and seventeenth centuries. There was probably no great demand for new cottages between the period of the Black Death and the destruction of the monasteries and as they were of timber, they had probably fallen into decay after the lapse of one or two centuries, and were swept away for lack of that tender care we sometimes give them now. Moreover, many more of the older have decayed and been taken down in the succeeding seventeenth and eighteenth centuries. We find, in fact, that the seventeenth-century cottage is now ripe for destruction, unless special pains are taken with it. I have, further on, stated which of the cottages I think may possibly be older than the sixteenth century, though my judgment is against such antiquity.

It was in the sixteenth century that the great change of ownership in land took place, and also the great change in the mode of life. Previously to this, many of the labourers on an estate had lived in the farmhouses and mansions, eating and, at

* Birch Cartularium Saxonicum, No. 521. Kemble, Codex Diplomaticus ccxcvii.

least in very early times, sleeping also, in the large halls which were the principal feature of the house.

About this time the old common hall life was done away with, and we almost invariably find the hall itself cut in two by a floor converting the upper part into bedrooms.

A good instance of this occurs at Tangley and elsewhere, as I shall point out later on.

The enclosure of the commons also disturbed the old patriarchal form of life and created a demand for smaller independent homesteads and for cottages on the estates of the great landlords, who entered upon the property of those abbeys and priories whose buildings had sheltered so many of the labouring class. As these ' nests,' to quote the well-known saying, were pulled down, room had to be found elsewhere for such of the cultivators as were retained on the estate.

An Act with some bearing on the subject is that of Henry VII., A.D. 1489, 'against pulling down of towns.' This is constantly repeated in succeeding reigns. It was directed against the wholesale destruction of tenements, consequent on the throwing of many parts of the country into pasture, and enacts that no house customarily let with twenty acres shall be pulled down ; it, on the contrary, gives special directions for its repair when necessary, under the King's direction in default of the owner's. This Act was probably not much needed in this particular part of the country, but it gives an idea of the class of house then existing and of the reasons why they have in so many parts disappeared.

We are informed by the Acts that the Isle of Wight was almost depopulated and had to be resettled.

At a later date, still greater destruction went on in order to get rid of the burden of poor-rates.

The statute of Elizabeth, A.D. 1589, is of a different character and has more bearing on the building of cottages. It is the statute that has been so largely quoted with regard to the famous ' three acres and a cow ' controversy. It states its object to be ' for avoiding of the great inconveniences which are found by experience to grow by the erectinge and buyldinge of great nombers and multitude of cotages which are daylie more and more increased in manye parts of this realme.'

The Act goes on to say that no one is to build, or convert buildings into cottages, without setting apart, at the least, four acres of ground to each. It excepts from this rule towns, mines, factories and cottages for sea-faring folk, under-keepers and others, and it also forbids the occupation of any cottage by more than one family.

This Act shows not only that cottage building was going on briskly, but that, just as still happens, old buildings were being turned into cottages as they fell out of use, owing to the erection of new and more commodious houses. Down to recent times, there does not appear to have been any great demand for more cottages and work chiefly consisted of additions of lean-tos, sheds and sometimes new wings and general repairs.

An immense majority of the cottages are of the date mentioned above and often it will be found that a prosaic-looking modern brick front is only the casing to the old building. It appears, however, that the custom of building timber frame cottages continued certainly as late as A.D. 1700.

There are a few older buildings, chiefly in the villages, that have mostly been converted at this date to their present form.

NEAR THE NEW STATION, GODALMING.

What I have said, as to date, applies to a great extent generally throughout England; but in parts, as in Kent, Sussex and the eastern part of Surrey, as well as in the Midlands, there are many more buildings of earlier date and especially of the fifteenth century. Architecturally the cottages are probably the better for being of this latter date, while the larger houses are less interesting.

In speaking of dates further on, it will be convenient to take, as the normal time, the period running from A.D. 1558 to A.D. 1625—that is, the reigns of Elizabeth and James I. It may further be said that the most active part of this, is the half-century from 1570 to 1620.

When, therefore, I use the words 'early' and 'late,' it is to be understood that I use them with reference to this period.

I must again guard myself by saying that, in the absence of exact documentary evidence, speculations as to date must be regarded only as probabilities.

A reason why cottages in this neighbourhood are particularly good, is that it was not a purely agricultural country.

In the southern part, or Weald of Surrey, on the heath-lands on either side, there were many ironworks and trade in wood and charcoal, and there was, moreover, at Chiddingfold, the earliest recorded glass factory in England, whence, as early as the fourteenth century, glass was sent to Westminster. There were also other later glass-works along this forest tract and there were old potteries and brick and tile factories.

Guildford and Godalming were old centres of the 'clothing trade,' where, in especial, blue cloths for the Canaries and elsewhere were made; Shiere and the adjacent villages were also engaged in similar trade. There were also fulling mills, and some of the earliest gunpowder and paper mills in England.

It will be found, throughout England, that it is in such districts that interesting domestic work of the humbler kind is chiefly to be found, while the cottages of a purely agricultural country are of little interest.

As I have said before, the architectural remains in this part are chiefly of the sixteenth century and there is very little of earlier date. Such as there is consists mainly of timber work buried in later additions.

There were few early important seats of families in the neighbourhood, with the exception of Vachery, or 'la Vacherie,' at Shiere, which was, in the fourteenth and fifteenth centuries, the favourite English home of the Butlers, Earls of Ormond. That, as well as many smaller mansions, has been entirely destroyed, while Loseley, the one important house in the district, is of sixteenth-century date.

In some of the earlier examples we find the remains of the Gothic style flourishing along with the newly-introduced Renaissance. Thus we have traceried bargeboards at Plunks, Shamley Green, Paddington Manor and Shiere, and, accompanying them, mouldings partaking of Renaissance character. There are doorways also, as at Bramley and the mill-house at Snowdenham, with the regular Perpendicular mouldings and stops, while the Tudor arch remains the usual form for the frame of external doorways.

Possibly, some of these examples reach back to the end of the fifteenth century; but in the great majority of instances one finds, even concurrent with some earlier forms, mouldings and carvings of clearly classic origin.

It is curious to find how rapidly this style seems to have spread itself into the most remote parts of the country. No doubt the many and extensive architectural works carried out by Henry VIII. had something to do with this. In this county there were built for him Oatlands and Nonsuch, near Ewell, and there were similar works of elaborate timber galleries at Esher Place and elsewhere. As these works were executed regardless of expense, and with great rapidity, they no doubt attracted mechanics from all parts of the country, who would carry back with them the traditions of the new style.

Professor Thorold Rogers, in his invaluable book on the 'History of Prices,' to which I am generally much indebted, tells, on the evidence of contemporary building accounts, that the joiners on Henry VIII.'s buildings generally had foreign names. Doubtless it was they who brought with them the new forms and doubtless, as in our day, the intelligent foreigner, once here, remained.

Other earlier buildings in the neighbourhood with a slight infusion of the new style were Hampton Court and Cowdray, near Midhurst.

Sutton Place, near Guildford, built in 1530, brought an early taste of the Renaissance and doubtless Loseley, commenced by Sir William More in 1562 and finished in 1568, exercised considerable influence on the art of the district, as his became so important a family in the county.

Throughout Surrey, also, we find, in parish after parish, records of the retirement hither on new-purchased lands, of old servants of the Royal Household, who naturally brought with them the latest ideas in architecture.

There is, moreover, a very simple and practical reason why the new style so quickly ousted the old. Up to the sixteenth century the demand did not exceed the powers of supply of skilled artisans; but if we consider the immense amount of building that suddenly went on in the sixteenth century and the consequent demand there must have been for workmen, it is not difficult to understand why tracery went out and mouldings came in.

The one required powers of design and skill of hand and plenty of time to execute; the other could be carried out, in half the time, by almost any workmen provided with the necessary tools. It would have been physically impossible to have erected within the time, in the Gothic or early Tudor style, the number of buildings that were actually carried out; and this, I take it, is one reason why the change of style was so rapidly adopted.

Building was very much expedited when square-headed windows and mouldings were introduced instead of carving and tracery.

At a later date, when the supply partly overtook the demand, we again get plenty of carving, but its absence is even then remarkable from the humbler buildings. The same cause is probably mainly responsible for the great degradation of taste at the beginning of this century, the demand for buildings having largely exceeded the supply of trained designers.

I take it that a similar reason largely accounted for the subsequent development of the Classic side of the Renaissance, to the prejudice of what may be called the Gothic half. Gothic and Elizabethan woodwork was pre-eminently handwork requiring individuality in the workmen, whereas classic detail was especially suited to the use of improved tools and could be executed without difficulty from the numerous handbooks in existence.

I have always thought that one principal reason why the Gothic revival, in spite of the enthusiasm and talent of its directors, has failed to make a permanent impression on our domestic architecture, is the unsuitability of the style of its woodwork to the trade of the joiner, especially since machinery has come so largely to his aid. The cutter of Gothic tracery, or Elizabethan rustications, is hopelessly lost in the struggle against the perfection with which Classic detail can now be turned out by steam power.

CHAPTER III.

PLAN.

THE normal plan of the oldest cottages was a simple parallelogram, containing one room on the ground floor and one on the upper floor.

Some of these still exist in out-of-the-way places, though it is seldom that they have not been added to and altered. Every day the number remaining in their old state gets smaller and smaller.

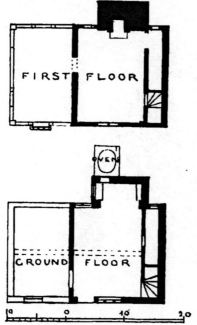

I am able to give two plans of cottages near Blackheath, on what was till recently the Grantley Estate. These had remained very much unaltered, until I had to repair and enlarge them for their new owner.

No. 1 cottage is of the smallest shape and retained, as is rare, its original winding staircase.

At an early date the part shown un-blacked was added to this. The oven is also an addition. I have never in any of the older houses or cottages found an oven that could be determined as of the same date as the fireplaces. The openings and brickwork are generally clearly additions and the flues are either taken up separately or into one of the old flues. As in houses of importance there were always two flues to the large fireplaces, this was the more easily managed.

All important houses had extensive outbuildings containing bakeries, breweries, etc., and when, as is common, we find traditions of wings, etc., that have been pulled down, I think it is probably these office buildings, which were less substantially built than the rest of the houses, that were swept away. For the reduced household, the earlier buildings would have been too extensive and the materials were doubtless used in repairs. Ovens were then formed in connection with one of the house chimneys.

There were, as now, bakers in all the villages, and most probably the cottager, unable to afford their bread, had to content himself with cakes baked upon the hearth, like those that King Alfred neglected and that are still familiar in the colonies under the name of dampers.

I give an illustration of a fireplace and oven complete, from some almshouses at Godalming. built in 1622 by Richard Wyatt, an eminent citizen of London and local landowner. These are now in trust in the hands of the Carpenters' Company. The exterior is illustrated at page 24.

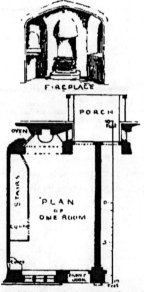

Returning to No. 1 cottage, it will be seen that it has the usual wide chimney opening with seats, though these latter are actually of later date. The opening, as is usual in all but the best work, is crossed by a large chamfered oak beam. In good houses, the first-floor fireplaces, being of smaller span, are generally formed of a Tudor arch in brick; but in humbler buildings, and garrets, an oak beam is used. In some cases, also, the oak fender curb remains, and in that case the hearth is made up level with the top of the curb and lies on the top of the beams and joists. In this cottage, however, the joists are trimmed for the hearths.

The arrangement of the partition in No. 1 cottage, which gives a large cupboard on each floor, also enabled a smaller girder to be used, and the length of the girder (which in oak is limited) naturally in great measure determined the size of the rooms.

No. 2 cottage has a larger plan, being in two bays. It has been divided on both floors, but certainly the upper, and possibly the lower, partitions are not original. The staircase was in a straight flight, a form of later date and in this instance of much later detail.

An early form of stair that might have been used here, is that where a straight flight is cut out of a solid balk of oak. Such a stair existed to the offices of Rake

House. Otherwise, all the earlier stairs were formed round a newel, and the modern form, in humble buildings, at least, is a sure sign of a date later than 1600.

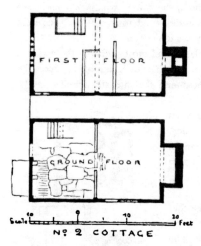

No. 2 COTTAGE

The unusually elaborate nature of the framed kingpost-truss of the roof of this cottage seems to point to an earlier date than usual, and possibly the chimney, which is built independently of the structure, was added afterwards. On the first floor of this cottage remains one of the open unglazed windows, usual enough in the older cottages, but not often found still remaining, except in barns and stables. They were formed by stanchions set diagonally and framed into head and sill. The opening was closed with a shutter. A window of the same sort is shown in the illustration of the small cottage at Dunsfold, p. 86.

One half of the ground floor of No. 2 cottage retained what was probably its original flooring of rough slabs of Horsham stone, fitted together like a puzzle. Brick paving, as in the other half, is always of a much later date. Where stone could not be conveniently procured, beaten earth was used covered with rushes.

Paving tiles were used commonly enough in the Middle Ages, but I know of none in this neighbourhood.

The adjoining cut of a cottage near Shiere shows a not unusual form of single cottage, with hip and lean-to at one end, and gable at the chimney end.

The long-curved struts, I fancy, are generally of rather early date. A plan of a rather larger homestead is that of Hawlands, near Chiddingfold, of which a view is given at p. 58. From the elaboration of the building one would take this to be fifteenth century, were it not for the classic character of the corbels shown at p. 58. There is a great difficulty in finding plans sufficiently unaltered to serve as types. In this case the part of the lean to left unblacked may be an addition, but otherwise the plan is original. There are here two rooms, parlour and kitchen, both with wide fireplaces. The stairs are in the usual position adjoining the large brick chimney. This is a position which may be called normal in the small cottages.

Ground plan, Hawlands

The upper story projects all round, except on the lean-to side, and this is a sure sign of an early date. This projection is carried by joists projecting each way and framed at the other ends into a large beam that crosses the room diagonally and projects sufficiently to carry the corner post.

This is constructional, but the effect inside is extremely unpleasant. These are called Dragon beams.

The piece of brick wall and the partition marked with 'notes of interrogation' seem to have been added to increase the lean-to scullery at the expense of the kitchen.

Since my sketch was taken I have received from the Rev. T. S. Cooper some further information as to the plan of Hawlands. The property has recently changed hands and the house is now being repaired.

In the centre of the front are now to be seen the jambs of what was, evidently, the wide front door. This is interesting, since precisely the same arrangement existed in the wing at Rake House, shown page 15. The door had in that case been modernized and I had doubts of its being in original position. It is possible that this wing of Rake was an older building similar to Hawlands and that the remainder was added to it; there are signs of independent building and this fact would account for the unusual position of the screen.

The old mediæval plan of a house consisted almost invariably of a central hall with an entrance and passage cut off from it by an open screen. Three doors from the passage led to a parlour, the kitchen and offices and a staircase. On the other side of the hall, doors led to one or more private rooms.

In this plan, the outside took the form of a large central roof with gables, or hips, to the two slightly projecting wings. The roof of the central part was commonly carried forward to the line of the projecting wings, so as to overhang the recessed hall. Curved braces supported the wall-plate of this projecting roof. An example of this may be seen at Compton.*

Often, the ground-floor wings have no projection, but the first floor of the sides is brought forward on projecting joists, as at Wonersh,† of which, however, one wing has gone.

The passage or entry, which was cut off by an open screen from the hall, was often continued out as a porch which had a small room formed over it, as at Nursecombe and Burningfold.‡

The best general account of houses of this class, with which I am acquainted, is given in a paper by the late Chas. Baily F.S.A., published in the Surrey Archæological Transactions, vol. IV.

There is, however, a form smaller than this original type and, perhaps, rather later in date, in which the plan is of an L or T shape.

I give a rough plan of Alfold House, a view of which is given on page 88. There does not seem to have been a chimney to the old hall, but one has been inserted with its back to the screen. A similar arrangement was made at Unsted Farm, shown on page 72. The Tudor arched doorways in these two cases are very similar.

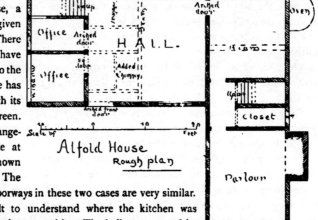

Alfold House Rough plan

. It is difficult to understand where the kitchen was situated in such a house as this. The hall was warmed by a fire on a central hearth, the smoke from which found its way out by a louvre, or l'ouvert. One can hardly suppose, however, that cooking, also, was done at this. It has been stated that wings have been pulled down at Unsted and Alfold, but there is no sign whatever of this having been done at Alfold. On the whole, I incline to think the kitchen was in a separate building, as was usual in early times, and that when the hall was made into a kitchen, this annex was pulled down.

At a still later-date, what had been a hall became the kitchen. Accordingly, we

* See page 70.   † See page 82.   ‡ See pages 79 and 86.

find the screen placed on the side of the hall next the private rooms. At this period the halls ceased to be used as the gathering-place of the whole family and domestics, and we find the old open-roofed halls divided by floors into two or more stories.

The plan of Rake House, Milford, which is annexed, is a good example of this smaller class of house. The outside is illustrated at p. 63. The plan is apparently that of the original house unaltered, as I had the opportunity of proving when restoring it. It had been but little altered, having been in one possession for the previous fifty years, and jealously preserved.

The windows on the ground floor, except some to the offices, had been put in at later date, and the only door that can be positively spoken to as original is that to the small building containing the stairs. As there is no sign of any fireplace in the offices, it is probable that the hall was the kitchen. There was the usual state room upstairs,

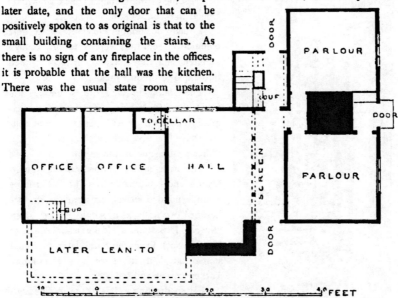

which probably served as a drawing room, and in this case had a very fine carved mantelpiece and panelling. It answered to the gallery of a larger house.

The staircase in the offices was one of those cut out of solid oak, and led to a small room over the end office ; from this, other stairs, that probably replaced a ladder, led from the landing into the roof.

This roof space was an example of the primitive garret, or cock-loft. Boards, laid along the centre, led to other boarded spaces in the centre of each gable ; these spaces were lit by small windows in the gables.

In no place, except the centre of the main roof, was it possible to stand upright ; but doubtless the boarded spaces received rough mattresses, or straw to form bedding for some of the household. The under side of rafters over some of these spaces

was also plastered, although that of the main roof was left open. In large houses one often finds that the top story, though only partly in the roof, and though provided with fireplaces, has the roof timbers unceiled and nothing but the tiles between the outer air and the room.

In some of the cottages I have drawn are similar lofts, but of still smaller size.

I have no doubt whatever these were commonly used for sleeping rooms, though at later date they have often been turned into apple or onion stores.

The stairs at Rake are somewhat unusual, the newels being of roughish timber, filled in at the back with plastering and ending above the first floor with a table top, a rather picturesque arrangement.

This is, as far as I know, an uncommon feature, and is interesting. The earlier stairs wound round a newel, or went up straight between two walls, as at Alfold House, given above. This stairs at Rake is intermediate between such forms and the later perfected stairs that had more or less elaborately worked newels and balusters.

I give a drawing and details of the fine staircase at Shoelands, near Puttenham. This place was originally a grange belonging to Waverley Abbey, but the present house was the home of the Lushers, a family of some importance.

There is a fine and unusual carved staircase in an old house at Shalford,* and one in the house by the church at Godalming, a replica of that at Abbot's Hospital. I believe there is a good staircase at Mitchen Hall, and there are probably many

* See page 95.

with which I am not acquainted. I give a detail of a very nice little staircase at Stonehurst, Chiddingfold.

It is to be noticed that the balusters at Shoelands and Stonehurst are not only

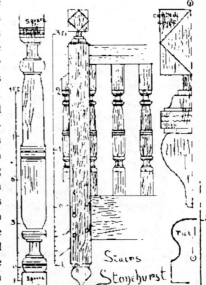

Stairs Stonehurst

moulded, but have sharp lines drawn round them in places. People are often puzzled why new oak-work looks so different to old. In all old carved oak-work, the surface is always powdered over with stamps of varying forms, and in turned work lines are drawn in addition to the mouldings. These give a softness and richness that cannot otherwise be attained, but architect and workman often fail to take note of these points, when repeating the old forms, and the result is, in consequence, disappointing.

The inside finishing of a room was of the simplest. In many cases, in the houses, the walls are very rough, being plastered between the posts. No doubt hangings were used to conceal the bare walls, and it is to be hoped that they were stuffed so as to keep the rooms warmer than they could otherwise have been.

Panelling became very general and was often treated as an article of furniture. The cottages are without these luxuries, but the farmhouses often have panelling half-way up. There are cases where the usual old fixed seat remains along one side of the hall and often the long narrow table that fitted to it also remains.

This is indeed a normal feature of these rooms at a time when chairs were not so plentiful. On the other side of the table was a long bench, such as those in Abbot's Hospital at Guildford.

Such seats and tables may be seen at Sansoms, near Baynards ; at Rickhurst, near Dunsfold, and at Shoelands, near Puttenham, and doubtless there are many more examples.

3

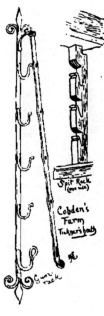

Spit Rack
(one side)

Cobden's
Farm
Tickner's Heath

Gun-rack

The ingle-nooks are familiar from so many pictures. Above the mantel-shelf there is often found a rack, which is sometimes erroneously supposed to be a gun-rack. A little reflection is sufficient to show that no gun could possibly be placed there. The racks were for the long bright spits in common use with the wood fires. On the mantel-board was sometimes fixed a piece of mechanism, often of elaborate construction, that turned the joint. One way of supplying the motive power to these, was by cord and pulley that communicated with a heavy weight outside the house. I know of no instances in this part, but in two farmhouses adjoining the church at Lingfield, in East Surrey, are two elaborate and wonderfully kept pieces of clock-work machinery for turning the spit.

I give a sketch of one part of a spit-rack of earlier and ruder character than those usually found, and of a gun-rack of iron, the only one I ever saw. A padlock at the bottom shuts in all the guns. These are both from Cobden's Farm at Tickner's Heath.

The question of furniture generally is, however, beyond my scope, and besides that, it has no particular local character.

CHAPTER IV.

TIMBER FRAMING, ETC.

NEARLY all the early buildings in this part of the country are timber framework, otherwise known as 'post and panel.' Brick did not come into general use in England till the end of the fifteenth century, and was for some time used only in more important buildings. There are instances in these parts—in Esher Place, built by Bishop Waynflete, and Sutton, near Guildford, built for Sir R. Weston in 1529. The chimneys are, however, generally built of brick and, indeed, as regards their common use, probably date from the introduction of brick.

Workmen, with whom I have spoken, have, however, taken down some old chimneys, the shafts of which were formed of wattle and clay. The latter had become as hard as brick. The Rev. T. S. Cooper has informed me of a similar instance along the Sussex border.

Rag-stone is plentiful in the neighbourhood, and was used for the foundations and bases of the frame. The stone found in some places can be fairly dressed, though chalk was generally employed for windows, doors, etc. Oak, however, was so plentiful that framing was generally used and the expenses of a mason dispensed with.

The frame being put together of oak, the panel is formed by fixing upright hazel-rods in grooves cut in top and bottom, and by then twisting thinner hazel-wands, hurdlewise, round them. The panel is then filled up solid with a plaster of marly clay and chopped straw, and finished with a thin coat of lime-plaster. The same system is used for inside partitions and occasionally the lattice is formed of oak laths.

In the older examples the timbers are large and placed so near together that there is quite as much post as panel; but, as time went on, timber became more scarce and expensive and the posts were put far apart and the panels enlarged. These larger panels were, in the better examples, filled with ornamental quartering, which is, I think, not found to any great extent before the latter part of the sixteenth century. These quarterings were cut out of the angles of crooked boughs and limbs of trees that would have been useless for ordinary building. In common buildings, and at later date, straight struts are often used instead of curved, but the effect is never pleasant. The main posts are 8 to 12 inches square, and the intermediate 6 to 8 inches by 2½ to 4 inches deep. It is the latter depth only that is filled up with plaster, except in the case of indoor partitions, which are commonly filled in, the whole depth of the posts.

Often the panels are filled up with brickwork, set in herring-bone fashion. The 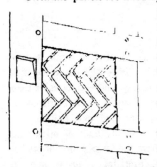 gray oak and red brick form a pleasing change from the ordinary black and white; but the effect is ruined if the timber is blacked, as I have seen done in modern work, as well as in restoration. This mode of filling the panels is, however, very unsuited to parts of a house exposed to the weather.

The blacking of the timbers is, in this part of the country, quite a modern innovation, though a useful and effective one where the panels are of plaster. The timbers have always been left un-painted, but it is quite possible this may have been only from motives of economy. The timber-work of Henry VIII.'s palaces had so much metal and gilding about it, that it must, I think, have been painted.

The notching shown on the face of the post in the illustration is generally found on the main posts, and, I believe, was made to receive the ends of supporting struts, while the frame was being put up.

In this district we do not find the elaborate patterns in the panels, that exist in some other parts, such as Cheshire. The principal ornamental figure is formed by describing a circle round the intersection of the timbers. Examples of this are found at Tangley, Bramley, Burningfold, Lythe Hill, Gomshall, and elsewhere.

In spite of this old authority, I think, for my own part, that it is better to design any ornament with reference to the panel rather than to the post. At this date and in this neighbourhood, the plaster is invariably finished flush with the posts. The plan often adopted now of keeping the plaster back about half an inch has the advantage that the face, instead of the back, of the plaster can be housed into a groove in the post; but, to my eye, it is very disagreeable. It certainly entails extra labour, and causes a difficulty with the cills, and I doubt if any old example of the practice can be adduced.* In older timber structures, the plaster is com-monly so kept back, but the edge of the timber is then invariably moulded.

There is an instance of this at Witley.

I confess the simpler forms of wood-framing are, to me, infinitely more pleasing than very elaborate and fantastic specimens such as are found in the North of

* I have since noticed an old example at Winchester.

England, just as it has been remarked that Elizabethan work is at its worst in its most elaborate examples. A feature particularly displeasing to me, is one never found in old work in these parts, but often introduced in new. This is the use of raking struts to the gables, at right angles to the rafters. The effect seems to me most distracting and destructive of all the value of the roof-line. I am aware that the feature is frequent in northern work, and it has an appearance of constructiveness that may probably be seductive to some.

I put forward the objection, however, only as my own opinion.

A distinguishing mark of older houses is the use, for the corner-post, of the butt of a tree, the spreading base of which is carved into a rough corbel to carry the story projecting above.

At the Crown Inn, Chiddingfold,* is an instance. The corner-posts often show the projection on the inside only, as at Rake House, where it is not used for ornament, and cannot have been of much structural use, and it has been suggested that the timber was placed this way that the sap might run out its natural road and the timber keep better.

The timber framing on the north and east sides of a building, is generally as sound and sharp at the edges as the day it was put up, though there are cases where the drip from the eaves has caused decay and where the bottoms of the posts and cills resting on a damp substructure, have rotted away.

These defects are intensified on the south and west sides, where often all that is left of the timber is the hardened skin and the very hardest parts of the heart of the oak.

The rotting of the ends of the posts has commonly caused the building to settle into all sorts of picturesque, but uncomfortable, levels. In restoring any timber building, the frame should always be raised to its original level by the use of screw-jacks. This can generally be done without serious difficulty. I had a large and fine timber house in Sussex, supported entirely on ten screw-jacks and brought back to its true level. On the other hand, if this precaution be omitted, all sorts of difficulties with floors, ceilings, etc., develop themselves.

Although it will always be difficult to render timber and plaster weather-proof on the south and west sides, there is no doubt the principal cause of decay has been the want of a damp course above the footings, and the absence of gutters.

It is in consequence of the decay of the timbers from these causes that the walls have been covered with hanging or, as they are called, weather-tiles. As far as I know, this plan obtains more universally in this part of Surrey than anywhere else.†

* Page 59.

† In Kent, the old cottages have, for the same reason, been very much covered with weather-boards, which have in great measure destroyed their interest.

It is not, I believe, of any great antiquity. I doubt if any of it be older than 150 years, and most of it has certainly been done during the last century. It is obviously not part of the original design, as the framing, etc., is always to be found complete under it and arranged without reference to its requirements.

The footings below the timber-frames are of the rough local ragstone, called Bargate, and in parts the black ironstones found on the heaths are used with it. In buildings of later date, the walls are sometimes built of this stone, as are the large outside chimney-blocks at an earlier period.

The joints, being necessarily rather irregular and wide, are 'galleted,' or stuck over with small black ironstone pebbles. The quoins are commonly of bricks.

In the seventeenth century, brick buildings begin to be put up in the towns,

and there are, in Guildford and Godalming, some very interesting examples of combinations of this rough Bargate and brickwork, of which I will speak later on.

Except in the larger houses, it is not often that there are porches to the front doors, though they are a usual feature at the back.

I give an example of an ingenious arrangement of porch from Brook.

The other, from Puttenham, is of quite late date and only given for its picturesqueness.

CHAPTER V.

CHIMNEYS.

ONE of the principal features of old cottages and houses in Surrey, is the skilful arrangement of the chimneys.

In this respect, this little corner that I am illustrating is, I think, equal to anything in England. In stone countries the chimneys are seldom a feature of interest, and although elsewhere more elaborate chimneys may be found on the larger houses, I know of no district where there is so much variety of the humbler kind worthy of close study.

There are two classes of chimneys: the inside chimney, showing only as a shaft appearing through the roof; and the outside chimney, which usually stands clear of the house wall and is of large dimensions and usually of ornamental treatment.

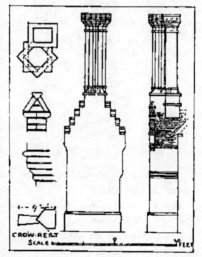

The base of these latter generally contains a chimney-corner or ingle-nook, or at any rate covers a wide opening, and the manner in which this is narrowed up to the shaft gives rise to an endless variety of picturesque treatment. The slopes are generally covered with tiles and the edge of this tiling commonly concealed by a parapet of 'crow-steps.'

The measured drawing I give of one chimney at Unsted Farm will illustrate this, and also one way in which the crow-steps are formed. A sketch of this house will be found opposite page 72.

Owing to the ease with which the top brick is displaced, these crow-steps have, in too many cases, been destroyed, and nothing but the square bases remains. It is astonishing how universal this ornament was. It will be constantly found attached not only to old houses, but on old chimneys to which most prosaic modern brick cottages have been added. The accompanying cut shows an unusual elaboration on the old timber-house at Gomshall, shown at page 90.

My sketches show a number of varieties of these outside chimneys, which might be largely increased by excellent examples, where the building attached is not so interesting.

I also give a sketch of the chimneys from Wyatt's Alms-houses at Godalming. An essential feature of these chimneys is the span-roof behind them. This sometimes serves to give headway to the fireplace inside, and in any case throws off the snow and rain. It is also most important to the general effect.

The mutilated ornaments in the head of the chimneys at Unsted are doubtless

the remains of 'crow-rests,' such as may be seen in the fine chimneys of Abbot's Hospital at Guildford.

They consist of a brick cut, where projecting, to a slightly tapering cylinder. A detail is shown on page 23.

Unfortunately, in building new cottages, one is generally debarred on economic and utilitarian grounds from the use of these outside chimneys, and there is perhaps more to be learnt from the treatment of what I may call the roof chimney.

One form of these is that in which the shafts starting from a solid block are slightly detached from one another, or are set diagonally. The first form is a favourite one at Dunsfold and Haslemere.

In another form the block has round arched panels, as at Abinger and Compton, pages 90 and 69. This form is not, however, common in the neighbourhood.

In some cases the block is simply ornamented by projecting the wythe, or division between the flues. An example of this occurs on the White Hart at Godalming, and on several of the Alfold chimneys.

Great strength is gained by this plan, if care be taken that these projecting wythes are built alternately solid and closure, and not all closure, bird's-mouthed to the block, as I have known done in new work. Most commonly the projection is square, but occasionally it is diagonal.

The projections of the head are carried round these wythes as if they were a shaft.

In the better chimneys these wythes are a brick wide; in other cases, and in modern work, half a brick.

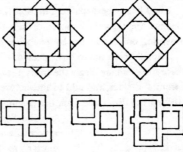

The greater number of roof-chimneys depend for their picturesqueness on the skilful arrangement of the flues, by which, instead of appearing as a square block, the shafts present a number of angles, thus gaining a variety of light and shade.

This is a great secret of the success of the old chimneys, and one that is seldom met with in new work, owing, partly, to the natural symmetry that results from the usual arrangement of cottages in pairs.

In the old cottages this disposition is not at all haphazard, but is the result of careful study of the points of view, and it is surprising what a variety of forms are to be found.

I give some examples, and many others may be found in the sketches.

The two succeeding plans are of a form very common in the Haslemere district, where the chimneys are unusually high and graceful.

The careful manner in which these lines of light and shade are studied, may be seen also in the arrangement of the 'star' shaft of the chimney at Unsted, illustrated above.

The charming effect of such 'star' chimneys formed by the crossing of two squares, is, however, best seen when the shaft is detached and the star complete; there is an excellent example at Wonersh.

I have given, on page 25, a diagram showing the jointing of alternate courses. There is some cutting to the 'sham corners' that can be avoided, by having three-cornered bricks made on purpose. The form then becomes a very simple one to build; but of course every white joint omitted is a loss to the effect.

Another feature to be noted in the roof-chimneys is the manner in which, when the ridge does not butt against the chimney-block, one side of the roof is prolonged above the ridge till it meets the chimney. The necessity for a gutter between the ridge and the chimney is thus avoided. A striking instance of this is to be seen on the cottage at Eashing, shown on page 65, and in a modified degree it is a constantly occurring and generally picturesque feature.

The flues of the larger outside chimneys are 18 inches by 18 inches, or 14 inches by 14 inches, and of the roof-chimneys 14 inches by 14 inches, or 14 inches by 9 inches; but at Dunsfold are some very elegant shafts, that can have only 9-inch by 9-inch flues. This small size is, however, quite exceptional.

I had better perhaps explain that the very slender shafts shown on many of the sketches are those of coppers, of late date, which are carried up in brick on edge, measuring only 12 inches by 12 inches outside.

A small point, not to be neglected, is the way a course of bricks is always projected where the chimney clears the roof; these courses come naturally at a different height at front and sides, and add to the picturesqueness and still more to the usefulness by throwing the drip clear from the flashing.

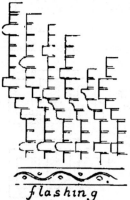

flashing

The flashings are of mortar, and must have been very ineffectual at first. Time, however, has given to mortar, as to tiles and bricks, a coating of almost invisible vegetable growth that effectually turns the wet. No new local brick will keep out the wet, and people are generally aghast at the quantity of water that may be absorbed by new tiles; they forget that old bricks and tiles were just as bad before they acquired this coating.

While speaking of flashings, I must mention an interesting survival of old ornament in the pattern drawn on them in the country districts with the point of the trowel.

This is shown on the accompanying cut, but it is, I fear, rapidly becoming extinct.

The heads of the sixteenth and seventeenth century chimneys are usually carefully formed of projecting bricks, the number of which and the arrangement, vary with the size and importance of the shaft. As a general rule the bricks are square, but occasionally, and especially about Shiere, simply moulded bricks are used. These are the half-round for neckings, the quarter-round, and the cavetto. I give a few examples of heads.

It must always be remembered that the old bricks are thinner than the usual modern brick, and that if these heads are repeated in our large bricks, the effect is so much too heavy as to become grotesque. This difficulty is generally surmounted by greatly reducing the projection, or by using moulded bricks. For the same reason it is dangerous to let the heads follow the projections of the wythes, as is usual in the old chimneys. If the wythes be allowed to die into the heads, support is given to what might otherwise look top-heavy, and a considerable saving effected in mitres.

The length of the older bricks is $9\frac{1}{4}$ inches, the width $4\frac{1}{4}$ inches, and the usual thickness is only 2 inches, and they are used with a $\frac{1}{2}$-inch white mortar joint. The beauty of old brickwork depends largely on these $\frac{1}{2}$-inch white joints. It is not only the small size of the bricks, but still more the large size of the joints that gives the effect that it is so impossible for that reason to achieve in modern work.

I have known great disappointment caused in cases where thin bricks had been specially made, but where the joints had not been kept the proper thickness.

I generally use a brick—still made in the neighbourhood—that scales only a full $2\frac{1}{2}$ inches thick. It therefore allows a $\frac{1}{2}$-inch joint in the 3-inch course, and the effect of brickwork so executed is vastly better than that made of the larger bricks. I have come across several amusing instances in which builders, and even surveyors, could not be persuaded that it would not take more of these than of the thicker bricks to do a given piece of work. The fact, of course, being that the quantity of bricks is the same, but the amount of mortar necessary is greater.

The importance of the wide white joints has been fully recognised of late in the charming drawings of Mr. Herbert Railton, and others, who have made it a leading feature. I observe, however, a tendency in less expert followers to exaggerate this feature to the extent of drawing the joints nearly an inch.

The bricks at Unsted are about $2\frac{1}{4}$ inches, and those of the chimneys of Abbot's Hospital, at Guildford, are the same, 36 courses measuring 8 feet.

In some houses at Puttenham, dated 1685, the bricks measure $8\frac{3}{4} \times 4\frac{1}{4} \times 2\frac{1}{4}$ inches, which is the standard size of bricks of that date.

Text-books say that an Act of Charles I., in 1625, regulated the size of bricks, but I have been unable to find the reference.

I do not think chimney-pots were used on the old chimneys, but the hoods of brickwork, often met with, may be of old date.   Later on, chimney-pots were used, and the ornamental heads reduced to two or three courses at most.

I confess that, to my eyes, pots are a great addition to the chimneys.

On the head of a chimney at Shiere is the date 1620, and I conclude with Mr. Baily, that that is about the date of the more graceful and ornamental shafts, the earlier being rather plainer in character.

I have already stated that the wide chimney opening was most often spanned by a chamfered oak beam ; less frequently there was an arch of brick, as at Rake House. The hearth was an open one for burning wood, and iron dogs were used for support-ing the logs.

These are often of local manufacture and of excellent character, though the best have now been almost entirely collected and redistributed.

Cast-iron fire-backs of bold character, with the arms and monogram and date of the owner, were not unfrequent, especially along the Sussex border.   These large, early, rude fire-backs are much more scarce than the smaller kind of more finished design.   These latter came from Holland or Flanders, and represent Scriptural or allegorical subjects, or the arms of one of the States, or a vase of flowers.   Some fire-backs probably came into Sussex from France, and I have seen a head of Henri Quatre that formed part of one.   Those who have these old ingle-nooks to deal with, generally find the greatest difficulty to get the fires to work properly without smoking. One plan is to let the wood ashes accumulate in a great pile until the fire is half-way up the chimney.   Another plan is to take a hint from what may be seen in almost every old cottage, and run a little curtain along the arch.   The effect is the same, the in-draught is brought nearer the burning wood.   These plans may mitigate the evil, but it is doubtful if they will entirely stop it, especially in houses where there is not the draught that the open door of the cottage often supplies.

I cannot resist a digression on the subject of beams running into hearths and near fires.   They are generally supposed to be the causes of the terrible fires that yearly reduce the list of our old houses.

A more probable reason, I think, is this : It is very difficult to get a satisfactory fire in these large fireplaces, and it happens that owners see at exhibitions or else-where some admirable new grate which they purchase and send down.

A local workman, or builder, is instructed to fix it, which he does by building thin brick sides as high as he can reach up the chimney.   An immense cavity is, however, necessarily left above, and generally at back and sides, since only enough brickwork is used to fix the grate in. Soot is then formed, and gradually fills up the cavities round the grate.

Next year, when the fires are lit, the immense heat developed by these grates gradually sets fire to the soot, which burns until sufficient heat is developed to set fire to the floor beams. I have known of a case where an incipient fire could not be traced until the stove was torn out, and such a heap of inflamed soot as I have described, disclosed.

It is most important that the spaces around grates fixed in old openings should be filled up solid.

CHAPTER VI.

ROOFS, BARGEBOARDS, ETC.

THE chief feature of a cottage must always be its roof, and it is the treatment of this that is all-important. Perhaps the picturesque result from the skilful arrangement and grouping of roofs of various sorts is the chief lesson to be learnt from old examples, since modern plans can hardly be made to agree with the old.

I have already insisted on the importance of simplicity. My sketches are necessarily taken from such buildings as have some shape, but there are hundreds of charming cottages that consist of simple parallelograms with plain unbroken roofs. The beauty consists in the just proportions, and the charm that is given by colour and by such glory of creeper as no architecture can ever emulate.

Beyond this first requisite, there are, however, many modes of treatment that are worthy of close study, and little tricks that add interest and piquancy to the whole.

The original roofs of cottages were, as I have said, generally perfectly plain, and the return gables and lean-tos that form such picturesque masses are therefore to great extent the result of accident ; none the less are they worthy of study.

The normal form of the roof of a house was something like that at Milford.*

The high roof here covers the hall, the larger gable the private rooms, and the smaller the offices. This house is itself of the later period, as the hall is built from the first with a story over it.

An older example is that at Compton, page 70. This is quite a typical form of roof illustrating what I have said at page 13 of the custom of bringing forward the roof of the central hall. In this form the roof over the wings is hipped instead of being gabled.†

The large steep-pitched hip-roofs, such as that to the Inn at Witley, page 61, are,

* See page 64. † The dormers in this roof are modern.

I think, generally of early date. The pitch of a roof is indeed an almost sure index of its date. Those of the time of Elizabeth are seldom steeper than about 48 degrees, while those of early date as constantly approach 60 degrees.

A very simple and effective form of roof for cottages, where the plan is a parallelogram, was used largely at the later part of my period and consists of a plain roof hipped at each end.

The hips are generally continued down to form the roof of lean-tos at each side, and the main roof is con-

tinued at the back for a similar purpose. I give a good example from Compton of such a roof. The back of this cottage will be found at page 69, and there are other variations of it from Farncombe and elsewhere.

This is the simplest of forms, and one most suitable for ordinary use on a pair of cottages, and yet one would seldom be allowed to carry it out. It must be noted, however, that the proportions are carefully studied, and the appearance owes something to such little 'dodges' as the way the hips are worked, and the manner in which the roof is connected with the chimney.

A feature to be noted in all the hips is the manner in which the top is formed by leaving a small gablet. In all old roofs no ridge-board was used, but each pair of rafters pinned together at the top. It was therefore obviously inconvenient to run the hip-rafters together to a point, and they were therefore run, each, to about nine inches below the junction of the pair of rafters. This, of course, caused the little gablet which certainly gives spirit to the roof, and in the absence of specially-made end ridge-tiles, had other advantages.

The same thing will be found invariably done with haystacks, the difficulty of forming the point being thus avoided.

Another point about old hip-roofs is, that the side always starts at a higher level than the front, so that the two dripping eaves do not meet at the hip.

Another form of cottage roof is that shown from Cranleigh, Dunsfold, and Chiddingfold,* which are variations from the same type.

The artful manner in which a gablet is formed to the lean-to at Cranleigh is worth notice.

* See pp. 85, 86, 59.

A very prevalent form of roof throughout England, at this period, is little found in this district, and one of the only instances I know of it, is at the house at Guildford, in the Woodbridge Road, page 97. In this form, roofs of smaller span are projected from the main roof, having their ridges at the same level.

These roofs finish in gables so arranged as to stand slightly apart and a short distance from the ends of the main roof. The springing of these roofs is necessarily above that of the main roof. The whole roof is thus reduced to a series of valleys.

This is a form that obtains particularly in stone countries, where it is almost universal.

The ridge-tiles are generally simple bent tiles, and there are a few instances only of what seem to be ancient crested ridges.

All sorts of fancy ridges were in existence at this time, but have not found their way here.

The roofing material is usually tile, but on the borders of Sussex and in the Weald generally, stone slates are commonly used, and in buildings of importance these are found further up in the county. It is probable that these stone slates were chiefly used and have been supplanted by tile in later years. Some of these Horsham slates are probably the original roofs, but it would be difficult to find an original tile-roof as, owing to the decay of the lathing, the tiles have in most cases been relaid.

Probably thatch was largely used before tiles, as was commonly, and is still, the case in Kent.

Bricks were very little made in England before the sixteenth century, and although tiles had constantly been made it is probable that they were expensive as compared to thatch.

There is a statute of Edward IV. laying down rules for the making of tiles and specifying sizes.

Doubtless, when the manufacture of bricks was added to that of tiles, and when the impetus was given to building, the manufacturer had a better chance.

The lath used for the tiles was, and is, of heart of oak, and would probably be still in good condition if it had not been for the splitting of the lath by the corrosion of the iron nails. It is a common thing, in stripping an old roof, to find the whole of the laths detached from the rafters and the tiling only kept in its place by its own weight. There seems to be no thrust in roofs of this pitch. I have taken down an old church roof where nearly all the tiles were loose, and where the rafters simply butted into a notch in the wall plate and were not nailed. Some of the ends had jumped out of this notch, but the roof stood although the situation was very exposed.

I ought to say that the roof was a very trumpery one, chiefly of sapwood, and was probably put up on the destruction by some means of the original mediæval roof.

The pins for tiling were of hazel or willow, but the delight of the tiler was to get hold of an old elder stump which was supposed to make the most durable pins of all. I have known all these woods used, though deal had generally supplanted them and is in its turn replaced by iron. The making of tile-pins was valued by the bricklayer as a useful occupation for winter.

The older roofs rarely, if ever, have dormers. The rooms are lit by little windows very low ar d near the floor.

These are very picturesque nestling under the eaves, and it is one of the great st difficulties now in getting the effect of the old roofs and cottages, that one cannot, for practical reasons, keep the springing of the roofs so low. These low windows were, of course, horribly inconvenient, and, later on, dormers commonly supplanted them.

If the dormers somewhat spoil the simplicity and breadth of the roof, they often add a picturesqueness of their own.

While on this subject of height, it may be as well to note that the height now often insisted on for cottage rooms renders them almost hopelessly shapeless, and in the country really answers no purpose, and is unnecessary.

Before leaving the subject of tiles I should like to give a final kick to a most obnoxious practice, happily now almost extinct, of using stained tiles for roofs.

Red tiles, especially ordinary local tiles, lose in a very few years the brightness so strong at first. They then improve every year, there being always sufficient of the red showing to give a warm glow to their colour. It must, however, be years before the growth of lichen gives them their greatest beauty.

On the other hand, stained tiles start brown and become a dirty dull greenish brown, and it is said that, owing to the chemical used, lichen will never grow on them.

Weather-tiles were hung on heart of oak laths nailed to battens, and were bedded in mortar. Work done this way is much more durable than it is when the tiles are nailed directly on boarding. The boarding, unless pickled, is sure to decay, sometimes very rapidly. Tilers, however, prefer it, as it is easy to get a neat, straight edge to the courses, which in the other way is difficult, owing to the irregularity of the laths.

I give a cut of various patterns of tiles. Pattern ‘B’ is that generally used. At Wonersh and Shiere, and occasionally elsewhere, are examples of ‘A,’ and I have fancied they had the appearance of being earlier in date than others. ‘C’ is, I think, only of modern date. At Haslemere are a great variety of patterns of weather-tiles, of which E, F, G, and H are examples not often found elsewhere, but ‘E’ is not uncommon over the Sussex border.

I have said that most of the weather-tiling is of comparatively recent date, but it is possible that some of this Haslemere work may be earlier. Professor Rogers mentions ‘wall-tiles’ in the sixteenth century, but it is not certain that they were weather-tiles.

Few things can exceed the glorious colour of old weather-tiling. The tiles retain more of their brightness than roof-tiles, while they have an equal share of orange and gray lichen intensifying and relieving their colour.

Of course nothing but age can give this and we must be content to wait.

What I have said about the use of stained tiles on roofs applies with still greater force to weather-tiles, and nothing can well be more offensive than to put alternate courses of brown and red tiles, as is done often enough.

Sometimes weather-tiling consists of all fancy-ended tiles of one pattern ; sometimes the courses are alternate, either plain and fancy, or of two sorts of fancy ends. Both these latter plans prevail at Haslemere, and both are very unsatisfactory, as all breadth is destroyed. There is, however, something to be said for occasional courses of plain tiling breaking the monotony and allowing the pattern to be changed. I do not myself care for the latter plan. An old arrangement of this sort in use among the workmen is five courses of fancy to three of plain. I think the gauge, or portion of the tile showing, should never be more than four inches at most, or the effect is poor.

It is most important that the three, or at least the two, lower courses of weather-tiling should be of plain tiles. This will be done as a matter of course by workmen familiar with the system, but in parts of the country where it is not usual the fatal mistake of beginning with ornamental courses may easily be made.

All local tiles are generally made slightly curved, so that the edges may grip when laid, and the most curved are picked out and used reversed for the lower projecting courses of weather-tiling. It is, in consequence, difficult to get the gracefulness of the old curves with Broseley or other accurately-made tiles.

The gable-ends of roofs overhang the walls, and were probably always finished with bargeboards.

Where weather-tiling has been applied to gables, the face of the front is brought to nearly the same plane as the verge of roofs; the bargeboard has generally been, in consequence, discarded and the weather-tiling finished with a flashing about two inches back from the verge of the tiling.

The greater number of the bargeboards in this district are moulded. Of others, there are two varieties: those in which the board is pierced with tracery and those which are cut into cusps.

I know none of this latter sort, except of a rude nature such as shown on several sketches and at 'D' in the accompanying cut.

In Kent and the western part of Surrey are to be found fine examples of the traceried cusp, but none of the houses in this district seem old enough.

Of the examples of tracery given, 'A' is from Paddington Manor, and 'B' from Shamley Green and from Plunks Farm; at the latter place it is carefully plastered up and only shows in one small place. 'C' and 'D' are from Shiere Village. The manner in which the junction of boards at the top is covered in 'B' is worth notice as very practical; 'A' is similarly finished.

These sketches show also the manner in which the beam forming the wall-plate was accommodated to the bargeboard.

There is a fine quatrefoil bargeboard opposite the Jolly Farmer, at Farnham. It has an indefinite line flowing round every pair of quatrefoils that takes off the monotony of those at Shamley Green.

I have never noticed this feature elsewhere, but it might easily escape one's attention. I give an illustration of this at p. 67 under the head of Farnham.

The houses having these bargeboards are certainly of earlier date than the majority of those illustrated, perhaps of the fifteenth century.

The bargeboards illustrated in the next cut are those from a house in the High Street, Godalming, illustrated at p. 74.

A coat-of-arms in glass points to a date anterior to 1537; but the mouldings would have made one expect a somewhat later date, and the glass might easily be older than the front.

'A' is the board of the dormer, and in this case the joint at the top is covered by a piece of the board fixed crossways. In the board of a corresponding gable the Tudor roses of 'B' are replaced by a plain chamfered circle. The bargeboard on the front of Nursecombe, now replaced by a clumsy imitation, was of similar pattern to this, and the old one at the back had a pendant similar to this at

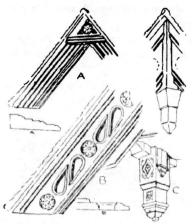

Godalming. The old front board, which is shown on my sketch, had no pendant at the apex, but old pendants to the wall-plate still remain, as shown at ' C.' These are an unusual detail.

Few things illustrate the reasons for the change of style that I have alluded to on p. 8 better than the bargeboards. This is also very marked in the mouldings of the joist-boards, or those boards or beams that covered the ends of the projecting joists.

At the earlier dates the ends of the joists were generally allowed to show, as at Paddington and Wonersh, and it was probably when timber went up in price, as it did very much at this time, that the joists became smaller, and the ends were concealed.

In the earlier examples, as ' A ' from Plunks, and ' B ' from an old cottage in Lower Lane, Shiere, these joist-boards are moulded on no rule, but apparently according to special design ; since, although mouldings somewhat similar in design

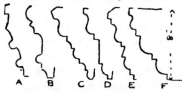

may be found, they cannot be said to conform to rule. ' A ' is a form found on beams of Henry VII.'s time, as in the north-east chapel at Godalming.

The others are a mixture of Perpendicular and Italian forms, such as characterize the early Renaissance. Either special planes or designs must have been largely circulated, since, although the collection of members varies, the patterns remain very much the same until the advent of still more classic forms, under the leadership of Inigo Jones and his school.

' C ' is from Nursecombe ;* ' D ' from the inn at Wonersh ;† ' E ' from Tangley,† and ' F ' from Hawlands.‡

* See page 79.   † See page 81.   ‡ See page 58.

CHAPTER VII.

WINDOWS AND DOORS.

IN the oldest houses, the jambs, sills, and heads of the windows are generally worked on the solid posts, but very commonly these have all been cut away and larger frames inserted.

Probably, in the course of a century, the sills had perished and something had to be done, and, as usual, it was found simpler, or suited the workman better, to put in a quite new window than to repair the old. Apparently, there was also a desire for more light; or, as is often the case, some of the numerous small lights were stopped up and a few larger substituted.

A very characteristic feature of the earlier sixteenth-century houses is the manner in which nearly all the spaces between the timbers of a room are glazed. This is shown in one gable at Tangley, and was the practice condemned by Lord Bacon, in the well-known passage in which he complains that one could not tell where to be to get out of the light.

These long ranges of light were very picturesque in effect, but the result of the window-tax, and the necessity of repair, has caused most of those in cottages to be closed. There are examples at Godalming, in Hart Lane, and the Waggon and Horses, Ockford Road. The lead quarries from the latter have disappeared during the last few years.

The older window-frames are always moulded, the earlier as ' B,' which may be called a ' Perpendicular' form, the later as 'C,' shown in the cut on the next page.

It is chiefly in the late insertions that one finds the square flat frames that have been adopted in some modern work, and that of high authority.

The windows of this detail are generally of very inferior work and design as to proportion, although in a few instances where they seem original, as in the house at Milford,* the proportions are more carefully studied.

It is true that in old work one often sees such detail looking well enough, but

* See page 64.

the moment one comes across a bit of the older and richer detail, one is conscious at once of the vast gap between the two.

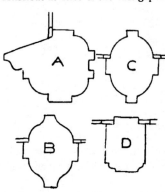

An exception to this is such square detail as that shown in the windows at the back of No. 25, High Street, Guildford,* where the 'squareness' is a strongly accentuated feature of the design.

While on the subject of detail, I must call attention to the almost invariable rule in the old windows, to give the transoms an extra projecting moulding, as 'A.' This gives richness and strength of appearance, and is very practical, as it serves to throw water clear of the lower part of the window. The extra thickness inside was commonly worked off by running a groove along.

The upper part of the transom was, and always should be, sloped instead of moulded. Trifling details such as this make an immense difference to the effect. Not only is the water thrown off more quickly, but one gets the form of the mouldings clearly marked where scribed on each side on the flat surface.

I may mention that the same rule applies universally to what one may call the sill of all old panelling. In that case it is the dust which is got rid of instead of the water, but the advantage from getting the expression of the mouldings is the same.

It is not till the mouldings are put in separately to the framing that they run round the four sides.

Another most important point in a transomed window is, that the upper light should be higher than its width. The exact proportion must vary with the total length of the window, and there is just one short total length where an exact square may be admissible ; otherwise, one may take it as an absolute rule, that the top light must never be a perfect square or wider than its height. It is necessary to insist upon this, since it is only too common to find work ruined by the top lights of long mullioned windows being made quite square ; this too in work whose authors ought to have known better.

The effect to a trained eye is every bit as distracting as notes played out of tune to a trained ear. A reason that helps to perpetuate the mistake is that if the proper proportions for external effect are preserved, the transom is apt to come about five feet from the floor, or just at the eye-line, which is unpleasant to those living in the room. Where this is unavoidable, the difficulty may be got over by dividing

* See page 101.

the short upper light into two, or two lights into three. In any case, to deliberately perpetrate a false proportion is as monstrous as it would be to go on performing on a piano that had got out of tune.

At Tangley Manor the windows are of rich and good detail, but in other places, as far as one can see, they were simpler, though the best of the old work has doubtless often been destroyed and only that of offices and back rooms been left.

Older cottages commonly have the upper windows set forward on brackets. The example I give shows two varieties. The original cottage consisted of the nearer part, being one square room with external chimney. The little window of this is of solid make. Another bay has been added to the framing and the corbels of the window in that case are cut to a delicate pattern out of board.

At Alfold,* Littleford, Sutton and elsewhere are examples of such corbelled windows and it is likely that they were the rule, but that, having decayed, they were replaced by common square section frames set flush with the wall. They supplied that delight of the cottager, a broad window-board, which was as good as a piece of furniture.

There is a good window of this sort close to the Jolly Farmer at Farnham, with carving, but I have never felt quite sure if it was *in situ :* it looks a little as if made up, but in any case is very successful.

The early doors are almost always formed of match-boarding fastened on battens; a very usual pattern is that given at 'A,' from Hawlands. There are variations of this up to 'B,' from Alfold House. Outer doors are often as at 'C,' from Godalming, the joint of the boarding being

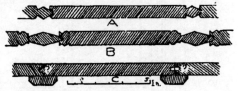

covered by hollow chamfered or moulded pieces, which generally run into a wide

* See page 9.

DOOR FORMERLY OPPOSITE TOWN HALL, GODALMING.

piece at the bottom and a piece of their own width at the top. These strips are often clenched to the boarding with large-headed nails. The whole door is strengthened by having continuous boarding nailed horizontally across the inside.

The insides of exterior and interior doors are in the earlier work left of quite plain boarding and it is evident were concealed by curtains. Where later panelling exists, the door is generally cut out of the panelling.

Panelling or 'wainscoting' was not a fixture, but was left with other furniture by will.

It is common to find that it has not been made for its present position, but adapted.

I give on the opposite page, a drawing of a very good door that came from an interesting brick porch that formerly stood by the Town Hall at Godalming. This was taken down a few years ago, and I was lucky enough to secure the old door and some interesting panelling

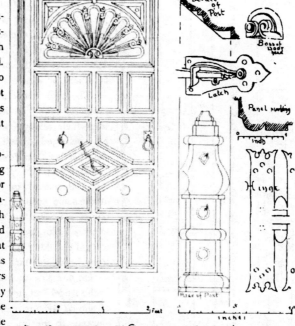

Door, Post & Details, White Hart Inn, Guildford

and fittings; these have been fixed at Ote Hall, a fine old timber house in Sussex that I restored for General Godman.

This house at Godalming was an instance of the manner in which old work may lie concealed. I had myself carefully inspected it, some years before, with the intention of buying it, and could see nothing but plain plastered walls.

When, however, it was being pulled down, from behind the lath and plaster appeared excellent oak panelling and mantelpieces of elaborate character over which battens had been fixed to carry the laths.

6

I have met with a similar top to that at Godalming at Elstow Priory, near Bedford, but in that case the door was of deal, an unusually early instance of the employment of that material.   This radiating top to doors was a favourite one at

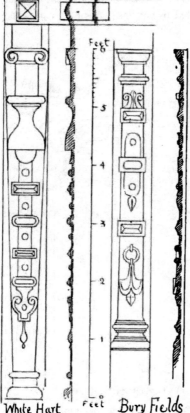

White Hart   Feet   Bury Fields

this period.   At Abbot's Hospital at Guildford is a series of splendid doors of this character.   There is one at the back of the White Hart and one at the old Grammar School of nearly similar pattern. Besides these, there is a fine door to the cottage at the Castle Arch and portions of another in Bury Fields.   This at the White Hart I give on the preceding page, as it is rather inaccessible and little known.

The door is not now connected with the posts shown in the cut, but I fancy, from their relative positions, they must have belonged to each other and that the door has been cut down to its present size.

The post here given is part of the frame of the entrance to the stable-yard at the same hostelry.   The other post is one of two forming a doorway in a cottage in Bury Fields, and from the style of the work, I should think it has been brought from the White Hart.

On one side of the carriage entrance to the Angel Inn are the remains of work of similar style, part of the original main entrance to the inn.   A disused window has its original glazing.   So much has been done to improve this ancient house that one would be glad to see a little justice done to this interesting bit of work.*

There are arched door-frames with carved spandrels at Nursecombe and Shoelands.

* This has since been partly done.

CHAPTER VIII.

GLAZING, IRONWORK, ETC.

A VERY favourite feature of old domestic work is the lead quarry glazing and it is a feature that has been seized upon and reproduced, perhaps, more than any other. Of its picturesqueness, both outside and in, there can certainly be no doubt, and when it is executed, as in modern work, with stout cored lead and with the glass firmly cemented in, there is not much objection on the score of comfort. The old quarries, however, were put into very flat and weak lead and though, I believe, they were sometimes put in with some composition of wood ashes, this has washed away and the windows fail to keep out wind or rain.

Unfortunately, the cost of properly made lead lights comes to about five times that of ordinary glass and rather more than that of plate glass ; it must, therefore, be regarded as an æsthetic luxury.

I may mention that the custom one sees, in London especially, of gilding the lead-work is quite orthodox, as the lead of the windows of Henry VIII.'s various palaces was so treated.

The two principal varieties of glazing in the district are the square and the diagonal. There are one or two ' octagon and dot ' patterned windows in Guildford, but otherwise I know of none.

The diagonal appears to have been universal at early date and the square almost so at later. As to their merits, I should say that while externally the effect of the diagonal is equal, or some may think even superior, to that of the square, yet internally its effect will generally be voted unpleasant from the distracting effect of the lines. It must be remembered also that the diagonal always looks the better on drawings, probably because its lines can be separated from those of the construction.

With regard to the shape of the quarries, it must be noted that they are never drawn with an angle of sixty degrees, as is commonly enough done in bad modern work.

Nothing can be more unpleasant than the shape thus formed. The older quarries were generally mote obtuse than the latter and in consequence much more satisfactory in effect. The sizes vary considerably.

The outer lines of the accompanying cut show a pane of ordinary size, but some of the earlier are nearer the square and better than this.

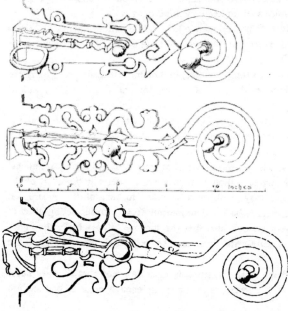

This pane is the only instance I know in this district of unglazed ventilating panes. The strap work is formed of a stouter triangular lead, the spaces between being left open. This example comes from close to Godalming, but in order that it may not be 'collected' I will not mention the exact spot. I think I remember seeing somewhere illustrations of similar panes from Sussex, where old work has been less destroyed than in this district.

The square, or more probably speaking oblong, panes are larger in size than the diamond and run from 5¾ by 4 inches up to 7½ by 6 inches, the larger sizes being of quite late date.

The glass in the older windows has generally turned a charming dull green, entirely the result, I believe, of decay. One cannot, alas! reproduce either any one or the variety of tints.

I must here put in a word against the prevalent trick of providing lead lights filled with quarries of different colours of 'cathedral glass,' under the impression that this is 'high art.' 'Cathedral glass' is a horrid material to begin with, and the collection of pink, blue, green and yellow squares, jumbled together haphazard, is about as vulgar a production as is often to be found.

The iron casements to which the glazing is fastened present a great variety of good work in the way of handles and of uprights fixed on the bottom piece. These latter are for the purpose of pulling the casement to, and are often pierced with a hole for the hook that forms the stay-bar.

The most elaborate series of window ironwork, that I know of, is to be found in the fine old house No. 25, High Street, Guildford.

I give illustrations of three of these drawn to scale. All the arrangements are not quite perfect, as the handles are now only dummies, espagnolette fastenings having been adapted to the windows.

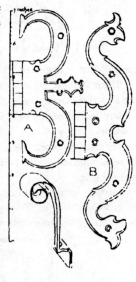

I show also the three pieces on the bottom bars belonging to these handles, numbered from the top.

This ironwork is, of course, of unusually elaborate character, but nearly every old cottage of early date has some good form of scroll handle. The flattened scroll shown below is a usual form for the handle to the bottom bar.

Undoubtedly modern iron casements are much more useful constructively, as they keep both air and weather out, but I wish that some of the principal manufacturers would take the trouble to collect a few examples of old handles and reproduce them instead of the clumsy and ugly types generally employed.

There are many examples of good hinges and other ironwork to doors, but of a kind common to the kingdom. There is a point about this ironwork that has not received due attention.

All hinges and such fittings were originally tinned and where a house has been well preserved and tenanted, the tinning remains perfect to this day; in cases of neglect more or less rust has eaten through.

This tinning, when it has lost its first brightness, gives the metal-work a colour not unpleasant to the eye, or out of harmony with the old oak. Modern reproducers of 'Gothic' ironwork, however, have turned out their specimens finished a dull black, which is, of course, 'impossible' for internal use and is one of many similar things that have brought discredit on 'Gothic.' Much the same effect, as is got by the tinning, results from the latest plan of nickel-plating on the iron, though this latter is, of course, a still better process.

The larger hinge—'B' in the cut on page 45—is of an interesting pattern. It

The Seven Stars

East Street Farnham

is generally taken to be founded on a cock crowing and the pattern is classic and of great antiquity.

In Archeologia, Vol. L., Pl. XXV., is a drawing of the remains of an iron-bound bucket dug out of an undoubted Anglo-Saxon tumulus. The handles of this have ends of the same motive as those of this hinge, and the interesting question arises whether the form is a survival from Roman times to the seventeenth century, or whether it was again introduced at the Renaissance. I think I have seen an illustration of a similar pattern among things found at Pompeii, but cannot verify this. The bucket to which I have alluded is now in the British Museum.

I had both of these patterns reproduced at Birmingham some years ago and I see that they now figure in some of the pattern books. Such work can, however, be well carried out by local workmen if they have the designs; or, better still, old examples to copy from.

Of good ironwork, such as is so often found connected with old sign-boards, there is unusually little in the district. At Farnham there are several examples, which I give.

Of other ornamental ironwork, there is a fine example of the last century in the gates and railings of Trinity Church, Guildford. There is also a good gate at Stoke House and other bits at Guildford and Godalming.

Iron Fanlight, Godalming

CHAPTER IX.

BRICK AND STONE BUILDINGS.

THERE is in the division a small group of interesting brick and stone buildings that are, I think, worthy of attentive study. They are very good examples of how to treat rough stone with brick dressings, and are of a more graceful and fanciful character than the later work when affected by the intrusion of Dutch taste under William III.

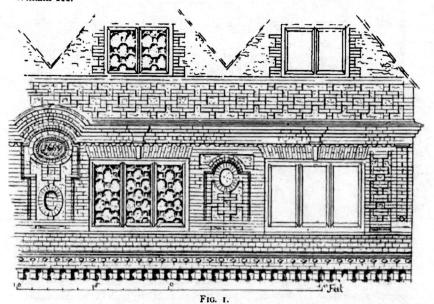

FIG. 1.

The most elaborate examples are two houses in Godalming, one of which is dated 1663. The other is evidently of very much the same date. The fronts of both have been painted, and it is therefore not so easy to make out the design.

No. 1, of which I give a half-elevation, had gables in the front that were probably similar to those still existing at the back, as shown in cut No. 2, or they may have been of ornamental brick, as in cut No. 3, since there is at one end of the main roof the remains of such a gable.

I am told that when, in 1840, the house changed hands, the top was finished,

FIG. 2.

as now, with a straight parapet all along above the points of the roofs. At the same time some 'octagon and dot' iron casements were put in the windows instead of the lead lights similar to those that still exist at the back. I show these modern casements in my drawing, as they happen to fit the building so particularly well that they are generally supposed to be the original design.

I give the backs of this and of the other house (cut No. 4) as good examples, and because they can only be seen from their own back gardens ; or, as I first

FIG. 3.

saw them, from the top of the church spire ; they are, therefore, little known.   It is to be noted that the projection of the strips of brick beyond the stone face is only from 1 inch to 1½ inch.

Most modern strip and panel work is ruined by the heaviness and coarseness resulting from the strips being made with 4½-inch projection.

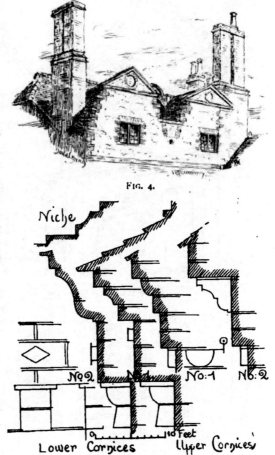

FIG. 4.

The other house, Nos. 3 and 4, is of similar character, but the arched recesses of the front are 2½ inches deep.

It is a thousand pities paint has destroyed half the charm of these buildings ; they are, however, still of great interest and specimens for a town to be proud of.

The cut No. 6 is of simple character and I give it to show a form of window head occurring not unfrequently in buildings of the kind.   The object of the half-arch was evidently to reduce the span of the flat gauged arch. Something similar is seen in the Farnham examples.

The examples, Nos. 7 and 8, are the two sides of what was the equivalent of a Town Hall at Farnham. The old front is said to

FIG. 5.

have borne the date 1657, and was of similar and very ornate character, but was taken down when the new Town Hall was built, and a plain brick wall was then put up.   The projection of the pilasters is 2½ inches, and of the panel work, 1 inch.

Besides these buildings that I have illustrated, there is a fine gabled and pilastered front to an old house at Shalford. This house has also a fine and unusual oak staircase and having been very intelligently treated in the way of repairs, is very interesting internally. I give an outside view of it and a view of the stairs, under the head of Shalford, at pages 94, 95.

There is also some good brickwork, of the same date, at one end of old Chilworth Manor, and the house at Abinger Crossways, just beyond my limit, is similar.

At the junction of the Station Road, with the High Street at Guildford, is a cemented gable with curved coping. This was one of three of brick, that belonged to an old house that stood here before the Station Road was brought through it.

From the garden of Abbot's Hospital a small annex is visible, with some rather elaborate brickwork.

FIG. 6.

FIG. 7.

FIG. 8.

7—2

The sketch from Guildford is from the very fine old house in the Lea Pale Road. This is dated on a gable 1658 ; it is a very fine specimen of simple work of the kind and is worthy careful study. The brickwork is treated as a wood frame, filled in with stone instead of plaster. This was a very large house, though many modern additions make it still larger. These were chiefly made when it went through the usual phase of a private asylum. It is now divided into three tenements, but I cannot help hoping it will some day be acquired by the town and devoted to public purposes, for which its situation and general character so well suit it. I cannot but think some judicious gutting and clearing would adapt it for some of the many uses for which accommodation is required.

The cut No. 9 is of a little garden-house that probably belonged to this house. On one side a cottage has been added. I give it as specimens of the sort are not common. The door between the pilasters has given way to a window.

FIG. 9

FIG. 10.

PART II.

TOPOGRAPHICAL

AND

PLATES.

CHAPTER X.

MAPS.

IN order that the topography of the district may be clearly understood, I have had the latest 1 inch-to-a-mile Ordnance map slightly reduced in size.

This will be the more useful, as this survey can at present only be procured by purchasing four separate sheets.

I have also reproduced that part of Bowen's Map of Surrey that refers to this division. This is of the date 1749, and is the earliest map that shows roads in a trustworthy way. Bowen was the re-publisher of Ogilby's ' Book of the Roads ' and no doubt had therefore had them under careful revision.

The map is valuable, because it is anterior to the formation of the new High-ways under the Acts of George II. and George III.

In addition to the roads shown on the map, there were, doubtless, open roads over the heaths; for instance, from Witley to Chiddingfold, over Wormley Hill. I see no reason to doubt, however, that the roads, as shown, represent the principal highways in use. The information printed on the map is taken from Aubrey's ' History of Surrey,' published in 1719.

The map next in date is the splendid map by Rocque, published in 1764. This is contoured in the most elaborate and careful manner, and shows everything. As, however, it is later than many of the new highways, it is not so useful a guide to the older period. I do not suppose any of the roads shown in Bowen's map vary from those of Elizabethan time.

I give also facsimiles of the road-maps from Ogilby's ' Book of the Roads,' showing the highways to Portsmouth and to Chichester through Midhurst. The original folio edition of Ogilby was published in 1675. My plates are, for the convenience of production, taken from the republication in smaller form by Bowen in 1749, entitled ' Ogilby Improved.' There is no difference at all between the two maps, except one or two trifling differences in the printing. Ogilby was, of course, the forerunner and exemplar of the better known ' Paterson on Roads.' Full information is given on all matters useful to the traveller. I have elsewhere enlarged on the principal variations in the routes

I have attempted to look into the Highway Acts, but they are among those not printed and exist only in the original Rolls of Parliament. As these rolls are each about 100 yards long, and one would often have to unroll nearly the whole with the chance of finding nothing of interest after all, I relinquished the attempt.

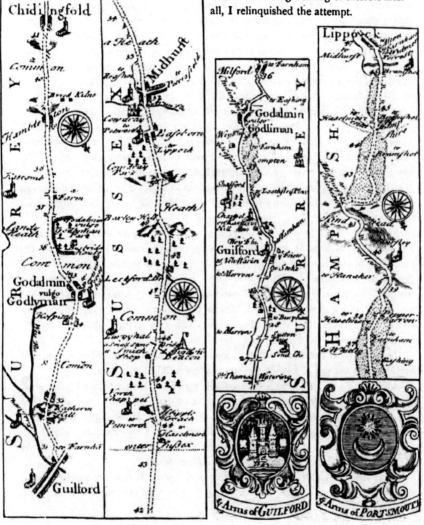

HASLEMERE: EAST STREET AND HIGH STREET.

Haslemere is a small town in the extreme south-west corner of Surrey, nearly at the top of part of the Black Down ridge. It is said to be the highest town in the South of England. It was, until the Reform Bill of 1832, a borough returning two members to Parliament. An Act of Elizabeth, A.D. 1596, in granting a charter, recites that 'the Borough or town of Haslemere in Surrey was very ancient and populous,' and that the burgesses had sent two members to Parliament 'from time whereof the memory of man was not to the contrary at their own costs.' The Act also recites a charter of Richard II. granting a market to the Bishops of Salisbury as lords of the manor of Godalming, in which Haslemere was included.

I have found one return previous to this date in the rolls of Parliament that have been found and published since the county histories were written. This is for 1584, when Christopher and Myles Rythe, of Lincoln's Inn, Middlesex, were returned. Most of the rolls from Edward IV. to Edward VI. are lost, and it is possible Haslemere may have returned members to some of these Parliaments; but it is far more likely that the privilege was conferred at this time for the purpose of packing the House with men on whose votes Burleigh could rely. The manor and borough of Haslemere at this time belonged to Sir William More, of Loseley, a trusted servant of the Queen.

It does not at all follow, as is sometimes thought, that places that sent members had therefore, at least at some time, been important towns. On the contrary, the conferring of the franchise was often a simple 'job.' An instance of this occurs in this county at Gatton where the privilege of returning members was conferred on the purely rural estate of Henry de Tymperley, a steward of King Henry VI., for the purpose of voting the marriage with Margaret of Anjou. The borough never consisted of more than the house and grounds. It is noteworthy in that the lady proprietress once returned the members.

Haslemere was the scene of tremendous contests between the different owners of property, and the roll of members contains many well-known names.

In 1784 the various estates were bought up at an immense price by that great Parliament-monger Sir James Lowther, afterwards Earl of Lonsdale; but after the Reform Bill, as they ceased to be of special value, they were soon dispersed.

There are here a good number of old houses, which I imagine are chiefly of the seventeenth century. The chimneys are particularly high and graceful, and chiefly of the form shown on page 25, or the square block form.

The house in East Street has a very dainty brick cornice of moulded 2¼-inch bricks: this certainly implies original weather-tiling over it, that can hardly be later than early eighteenth century.

EAST ST, HASLEMERE.

HIGH ST, HASLEMERE.

PHOTO-LITHO, SPRAGUE & Cº LONDON.

SHEPHERD'S HILL HASLEMERE

AT SHOTTER MILL

PHOTO-LITHO, SPRAGUE & C° LONDON

HASLEMERE : SHEPHERD'S HILL AND SHOTTERMILL.

The weather-tiles at Haslemere are of most varied form ;* indeed, this is the only part of the district where there is any great variety. It is possible that the very exposed position caused their use at an earlier period than elsewhere.

The cottage on Shepherd's Hill stands on the old road that went right over the top of the down, where, according to Aubrey, the old town was situated. The projecting hood of weather-tiles, with plaster cove under it, is a characteristic feature that will be found in other examples, as Combe Farm† and Tuesley.‡

Aubrey reports the tradition, that there had once been a town here which was destroyed by the Danes ; there was, however, certainly no place of importance in early mediæval times, and it is probable it owed its size to its representation in Parliament and the consequent creation by rival interests of fresh qualifications. There was once a crape factory here, and there are one or two mills in the neighbourhood, of paper and leather.

The house at Shottermill is curiously like a small version of Rake House, page 63. The small gable has the timbers filled in in the same manner, with herring-bone brick; there is here in addition some 'basket-work' pattern at the top. The end of the building is entered by a door approached from outside by steps, and was no doubt a granary. Such an arrangement is not at all unusual in old farmhouses.

Pitfold Farm

Pitfold Farm, beyond Shottermill, is a house of some character, the entrance gateway to which I give ; it is dated 1668.

About this part, at Critchmere, are a number of old 'squatter's cottages' of the very tiniest size. They probably housed charcoal-burners, iron-workers, or the glass-workers who were said to be at Hindhead in the time of Elizabeth.

Near Haslemere is its manor-house, which contains some old panelling and has some ornamented garden walls and other features.

* See page 34.   † See page 60.   ‡ See page 65.

8

LYTHE HILL AND HAWLANDS.

Lythe Hill is in the parish of Chiddingfold, and full particulars of its history will doubtless appear in a work on the history of the parish, now in preparation, by the Rev. T. S. Cooper, of Stonehurst.

There can be few more useful contributions to county archæology than such histories. It is to the diligent examination of old deeds, court rolls, and other documents, that one must look for further elucidation of the history of our ancestors. In default of precise information, it is rash to pronounce too definitely as to the precise date of buildings, a judgment that had better be left until we have the advantage of a large collation of ascertained facts.

Lythe Hill Farm has undergone thorough restoration, and it is impossible to tell how much is old or of old pattern. I therefore give it under reserve. I am assured, by the occupant, that it is old and it may very well be so. There is, however, one filling-in of a lower panel, with diagonal timbers, that is quite unlike the rest of the ground-floor or work in the South of England, and I think this must be an introduction. The room inside this wing is panelled, and there is a Queen Anne mantelpiece with excellent carving. The house was the property of the Quynell family, by one of whom this ornamental wing was built. It is evident that this wing has been added to an older house of the usual pattern with recessed centre. The pattern of the quartering is similar to that at Tangley,* which is the leading example of this class of house in the neighbourhood.

I have had to omit several trees that prevent one from getting a complete view of the house, and make sketching difficult.

Hawlands is a very interesting old house in an out-of-the-way place. The double projection of the upper story is a sign of early date. This projection is carried at the corners by large dragon beams crossing the room diagonally ; into these the joists are framed. A plan of the house will be found at page 13.

I give a sketch of one corbel, which is very roughly executed, but clearly in the new style. Had it not been for this corbel, I should have taken the house for fifteenth century.

* See page 81.

LYTHE HILL FARM.

HAWLANDS, CHIDDINGFOLD

AT CHIDDINGFOLD.

THE CROWN, CHIDDINGFOLD.

Chiddingfold: Crown Inn and Cottage.

This parish of Chiddingfold is a settlement of great antiquity. Within the last few years the foundations of a Roman villa have been discovered at Pockford, and I have pointed out elsewhere that the wide green road, known as High Street Green, was a Roman road leading from Castle Copse, on Black Down, to' the Roman camp at Hascombe. Mr. Cooper's researches confirm this suggestion. In the district were old ironworks, and, as I have stated, this has been regarded as the earliest recorded place for the making of glass in England.

This notice goes back only to the late fifteenth century, and implies that the maker is the only one in England. The Architectural Dictionary, in a learned article, gives the earliest record in England as 1446. I have, however, found entries of the supply of glass from Chiddingfold to St. Stephen's Chapel at Westminster in 1350, and Mr. Cooper tells me he has still earlier notices. Pickhurst is a house of character with some bold chimneys, which have the wythes diagonally projected. There are, about the large parish, many timber-frame cottages of early date.

The Crown Inn is a very old house, and has a fine fourteenth-century king post roof over what was originally the hall. The overhanging building at the back is canted off in a curious way, to follow the line of an old lane or passage. The porch is a recent addition.

Mr. Cooper tells me that deeds, that he has copied, speak of a building here in A.D. 1383, and no doubt the 'aula' spoken of is this hall. Another deed of 1548 speaks of the additions lately made to 'le Croune.' The spreading bracket of the corner-post is carved out of the solid, the butt of the tree being placed upside down for the purpose. The cottage above this is of very good form, variants of which occur at Dunsfold* and Cranleigh.†

A cottage adjoining has had half taken down, and shows the brick Tudor arches of its upper fireplaces that imply a sixteenth or early seventeenth century date.

* See page 86.　　　† See page 85.

CHIDDINGFOLD : COTTAGE, AND COMBE FARM.

The cottage at the top is of unusual form, and higher than is generally the case.

Combe Farm, from the steepness of one gable and some other appearances, seems to me as possibly of early date in parts; the near end is comparatively modern.

In the parish is an old house called Stonehurst or Stonehouse. It contains a nice staircase, some details of which I have given on page 17.

The present highroad to Chiddingfold comes from Godalming through Witley, but the original road came through Hambledon and continued along the present footpath through the Hurst.

The line is marked by a sturdy avenue of oaks. This is shown in Ogilby's 'Book of the Roads,' published in 1675,* as the highroad from London to Chichester through Midhurst. After leaving the county, at Cripple Crouch Hill, the road went by what is still known as Old Midhurst Lane.

This part of the road, through the clays, was probably a very difficult bit on what was notoriously one of the very worst roads in England, and when the new highroad was made over Wormley Hill, it was, no doubt, quickly abandoned for a connection with that.

It is most important in investigating the history of a place to consider the roads. These have, in many cases, been totally altered during the last century, and the effect has been to change entirely the relationship between various places.

Hambledon is an adjoining village at the foot of the Sandhills. There are one or two delightful cottages in it, particularly the old Malt House block. This is well known to artists as a most splendid specimen of colour, but it has hardly sufficient architectural feature for representation here.

* See page 55.

AT CHIDDINGFOLD.

COMBE FARM

AT WITLEY.

PHOTO-LITHO, SPRAGUE & CO LONDON.

NEAR WITLEY.

Witley : White Hart and Cottage.

Passing northward from Chiddingfold we come out of the Weald on to the ridge of sandhills that overlook it and to the village of Witley.

The present highroad over Wormley Hill dates, probably, from 1764, and I believe was improved on the making of the railway. Previously, the road coming from Godalming branched by the church to Brook Street, and by Colmar, past Sweetwater Pond, to Hambledon Parsonage.*

There was at Witley a park belonging to the manor, where, no doubt, the noble and royal owners came to hunt. The park was toward the slope of the Hindhead Hills. There is a moat near Stroud where the lodge probably stood Afterwards there were two furnaces for iron ore here.

The White Hart Inn has been done up externally, but not so as to alter its ancient character. These high and large roofs are, I think, signs of early date.

The cottage with the bow-window is also of early date, and I should think, most likely, is one wing of a better house, the rest of which has been pulled down. The character is something like that at Unsted. The framing under the lights of the bow-window is moulded on the edge, and the plaster set back, a sign of older and more careful work.

The Parsonage Farm, Witley, is of good form, temporarily disturbed by the brightness of some new additions.

Toward the Hindhead is a place called Emley that has a very old look, and there are various old buildings about the Heaths and at Thursley ; but, as I have already pointed out, the cottages and smaller buildings of such agricultural districts are not of much interest.

On the Hambledon road is Great House Farm. This was a square Queen Anne or early Georgian house, with immense farmyard in front, encompassed all round with a range of splendid barns. There was no such other set of buildings in the neighbourhood ; the need for them having ceased, two sides have been pulled down, and the house made much more habitable.

* See Bowen's Map.

WITLEY: COTTAGES.

At the time of the Domesday Survey, Witley was in the possession of the important Norman family of De Aquila or De l'Aigle. The manor then passed through the hands of the Albinis of Arundel, the Mareschals of Pembroke, Peter de Savoy, Warrens of Surrey, Clares of Gloster, until King Henry III. bestowed it on Prince Edward and his heirs.

It then seems to have become part of the usual dower of the Queens of England, and in the time of Henry IV. the men of Witley were, as tenants of the Crown, by special charter exempted from serving on juries. This was confirmed by Elizabeth, and the exemption has continued.

The ill-fated Duke of Clarence had a grant from Edward IV. of the manor, and an inscription in the chancel of the church records his connection with it.

Thomas Jones, one of the Sewers of the Chambers' to Henry VIII., had a lease of it from Elizabeth, and, through the hands of the Mores of Loseley, the manor was purchased by Henry Bell,* Clerk Comptroller of the Household to James I. From him it passed to his sister, wife of Henry Smith,† of Rake House, whose son and heir, Anthony, was Clerk of the Spicery to James I. His son, Anthony, is described on his tombstone as 'Pentioner' to Kings Charles I. and II.

I mention these particulars of the descent of this manor as an instance of the character of the ownership at various periods; I have elsewhere alluded to the numbers of old Court servants who invested their savings in Surrey.

The great families who owned the various manors, previous to the break-up in the sixteenth century, must have considerably influenced the history of their possessions, though probably, with the exception of the Butlers of Shiere, they rarely came near them.

It was the advent, into the sleepy old country places, of the active men of business and affairs, with capital to lay out, that did much to make England what she has become. Unfortunately an amount of mischief and injury was done to the country folk, from which we suffer still.

The cottage by the church is a favourite subject for artists, and has, I should think, been as often drawn as anything in England.

The cottage, with two half-hips, is a good example of a very simple form; as will be seen, there is a room in this roof that must be of very limited space, such as I have alluded to on page 16.

---

* In 1614; he was of a Glostershire family.

† Henry Smith was the son of Anthony Smith, a member of an old family of Escrick, Yorkshire. Several important families of the name have the same coat of arms. This Anthony married the daughter of Thomas Harward of Hall Place, Merrow. Manning incorrectly gives this name as Howard.

AT WITLEY.

AT WITLEY

RAKE HOUSE.

RAKE HOUSE.

RAKE HOUSE.

Rake House is an interesting specimen of an Elizabethan house; I have given a plan and some particulars at page 15. It belonged to the Smith family, lords of the manor of Witley, of whom particulars are given on the preceding page. On one of the carved mantelpieces are the initials H. B. and the date 1602. John, the father of Henry Bell, is described as of Milford, and it is probable that the house belonged to him and was added to, or at any rate beautified by, Henry Bell. This Henry died in 1634, aged eighty years. We have no record of the death of his brother-in-law Henry Smith, but it is probable that he was already dead, as a very large and fine iron fire-back in the hall bears the initials H. B. and A. S., and the date 1630; the model for the letters has been made the wrong way, so that they have come out reversed. A broken example of the same fire-back was found in a neighbouring cottage. It appears, therefore, that at this time, Anthony, son of Henry Smith, was living with his uncle.

The lower and upper rooms of the wing on the porch side were panelled with very good oak and had extremely good carved mantelpieces. This carving is of well-designed and delicate character, and not rude as is often the case at this date. The upstairs room corresponded to the gallery of a large house, and was, no doubt, the withdrawing room. The arches of the fireplaces are of brick and Tudor-shaped, and on the plaster jambs, when opened, we found roughly executed arabesque scrolls in distemper. These, however, were neither distinct enough to preserve nor to trace.

The lean-to, on the chimney side, is an addition to the house; the gable on the main roof was repeated on the opposite side, but had been destroyed.

In the windows were some good armorial panes of glass as follows:

On large ovals, with helmets and rich mantlings; No. 1, the coat of Anthony, son of Henry Smith; arg. a bend az. between two unicorn heads erased az. for Smith, quarterly with arg. a chevron gu. with three bars gemelle between three hawk's bells, for Bell; crest, a unicorn's head out of a coronet. No. 2, Smith as before, but the bend is charged with three lozenges bendwise Or (omitted on the previous coat only); the crest is a demi-bull out of a ducal coronet, being that of the Yorkshire family. No. 3, the coat of Anthony, father of Henry Smith; Smith impaling az., a lion ramp. arg., over all on a fess, Or, three roses gu. for Harward (of Merrow); crest double, a demi-bull for Smith, and a demi-stag ducally gorged and attired for Harward. No. 4, a large shield, Smith impaling Harward. On small quarries No. 5, the arms of Henry Smith; Smith (with a mullet sable as third son of Anthony) impaling Bell (the chevron not coloured), labelled Smith, Bell. No. 6, the arms of Anthony, grandson of Henry Smith; Smith impaling, sable bordered Or three cinquefoils arg. pierced gules, labelled Hoare (of Farnham, but the coat will be found under Hore, co. Warwick). No. 7, the coat of Anthony, son of Henry, Smith (with the mullet) impaling Or three bars gu. for Muschamp (of Peckham), first wife. No 8, Smith, as before, impaling sa., a cross potent Or, for Allen, for the second wife of Anthony, labelled Smith, Allen. The bearing of Allen in the church is given by Manning as a cross patonce, probably by mistake; the family were from Essex. (These coats have now been brought together in the hall.)

On the east side of the house is a large square garden enclosed by a fine stone wall; the entrance was in the centre of this; on the other side of the house is a mill-pond, the extent of which has since been curtailed. In the grounds is a square stone pigeon-house with four gables; both house and pigeon-cote are conspicuous from the railway. There was some half-panelling in the other sitting-room, but the rest of the oakwork is imported. I have given a particular description, as the house is not mentioned in the county histories.

SANDHILLS AND MILFORD.

The cottage at Sandhills is one of several of interest that lie along what seems to me to have the appearance of a very ancient road, running along a ridge from east to west.   The old road from Witley joins this road at Brook Street, where is a little collection of cottages.   One of them, though a good deal altered, still shows the upper story projecting all round, and I have been told that the bargeboard, lately on the porch of Witley Church, was brought from this cottage.   It is of the simple cut cusp form, as on Alfold House* and Shamley Green,† and the framing of the gable is similar to that of those houses.   I have shown on page 22, part of another old cottage, rather further on the road, that has a clever arrangement of porch and verandah.

The house at Milford is of a very typical form.   It has the large roof over the hall in the centre and the gable at each end.   The one contains the sitting-rooms, and the other the kitchen and offices.   The hall in this case has ceased to extend to the roof, but is built with a story over it.   The windows here are original windows of square section, some similar instances of which are to be found in some of the old houses about Shalford.

This house is covered, not with nice comfortable rough cast, but with smooth cement, which does not do it justice.   It is also almost obscured from view by two very large yews.   These, probably, began life as humble peacocks, but have grown into veritable upas-trees, overshadowing the house completely.   It is always a hard struggle to sacrifice a fine tree, but at least one of these might be spared with advantage to the appearance and the healthfulness of the house.

At Moushill is an old manor-house that had the honour of being restored by Pugin.   He also executed, for Viscount Midleton, some beautiful work at Peperharow Church, the entrance to the park at Oxenford Grange, and a vaulted building over Bonfield springs.   There is at Moushill an ingle-nook and a very low heavily beamed hall.

Near here is a cottage with an interesting brick front, copied from that of an old house that stood in the High Street, Godalming, the door from which I have given on page 40.

The house at Peperharow was built by Sir William Chambers, the architect of Somerset House; the grounds were laid out by Capability Brown.

Milford House was built in the last century by Thomas Smith, of Rake House From him it passed by marriage to the Webb family, who now own it.

* See page 88.   † See page 84.

AT SANDHILLS, WITLEY.

AT MILFORD.

PHOTO-LITHO, SPRAGUE & Cº LONDON.

AT TEWSLEY.

PHOTO-LITHO, SPRAGUE & Cº LONDON

AT EASHING

TUESLEY AND EASHING.

The cottage at Tuesley has a conspicuous example of weather-tiling projected to form a hood. This gives a good deal of character to an otherwise perfectly simple building, and is an instance how sufficient it is, in a building of this sort, to confine one's self to one feature and not crowd in too many, to the prejudice of economy and appearance.

Tuesley, or, as sometimes spelt, Tewsley, is a little settlement probably of great antiquity. Kemble thinks the name commemorates the Saxon god whose name survives in 'Tuesday.'

There are old foundations about, and walls that have an old look, and the sides of the hill adjoining seem to show signs of terrace cultivation. In Chapel Field, on a hill close by, were the foundations of an old church and burial-place, described in a grant of Edward VI. as 'the chapel called the old Mynster with the burial ground.' The name Mynster is a sign of at least Saxon date, and what has been recovered of the plan suggests a very early building that may have taken the place of the grove or building, sacred to the Saxon or Belgic god. That, again, may have occupied a still older site.

The view of the cottage at Eashing shows the back. The roof is continued down to cover offices behind the principal rooms. A particular feature of this cottage is the way the roof is carried on, beyond the ridge, to meet the chimney block. This is an invariable form where required by the position of the chimney, but is not often so marked as in this instance. From the opposite side, the chimney-stack looks unusually high in consequence. There is here an interesting old shed to a well, with old wheel and bucket.

At Eashing was Hall Place, the house of the Richard Wyatt who built the Alms-houses at Godalming; this has been taken down. Near Eashing House is a brick and timber building with circle work in the gable. This has been taken to be part of Hall Place, but is on the estate formerly called Jordans, that belonged to the Tichbourne family.

FARNHAM.

Farnham is a place of great antiquity, though its claims to figure in the Itinerary of Antoninus are yet unsettled. It is certain that besides earlier camps there were extensive Roman settlements all around it, as at Bentley, Crondall, and Tongham. It lies at the junction of two important roads. One came from Winchester, the capital of the West Saxon kings, and the place where the treasury was kept in much later times; this road also led to the port of Southampton. Another important highway was that coming from the west and passing to Kent along the Hog's Back. In medieval times an immense stream of pilgrims used to come from Normandy to Southampton and pass through Farnham and along the Pilgrims' Way to Canterbury.

We learn from charters that Farnham early formed part of the West Saxon kingdom, and this and the fact of its being handed over to the Bishopric of Winchester, have always kept this Hundred rather distinct from the rest of the division and of Surrey.

Another sign of the wildness of the country is the foundation here in 1128 of Waverley, the first Cistercian abbey in England. The Cistercian order, as is well-known, were the great pioneers of agriculture and their houses were always founded in out-of-the-way and wild districts. They held, in later times, numerous possessions about this and neighbouring counties, and the scattered positions of their properties must have necessitated constant travelling and keeping up of roads. Professor Rogers has shown that roads in the Middle Ages were, owing partly to this cause, in good condition, and that carriage was cheap and easy. It was not till the destruction of the religious bodies and the general change of proprietorship that the roads fell into such a bad state as the last century found them in.

At the Reformation, the estates of Waverley passed into the hands of Fitz-William, Earl of Southampton, from whom they came to Antony Brown, Viscount Montagu of Cowdray. The properties in this division were, however, quickly disposed of, and chiefly to Sir George More. Little remains of the Abbey but the ambulatory. The house above was the work of Campbell, a somewhat famous architect in his day.

Farnham returned two members to Parliament in 1311, 1312, and 1460. These were, doubtless, cases of packing with the Bishop of Winchester's nominees. The first and second dates were the occasions of the presentation by the Barons, to Edward II., of ordinances directed, in great measure, against the favourite Piers Gaveston.

The second occasion was when Parliament met for the declaration of Edward IV. as king, after the defeat and capture of Henry VI. at Northampton.

Farnham is stated by Aubrey to have been one of the greatest wheat-markets in England, but in later times the trade was transferred to Guildford, probably after the improvement of the highways out of Sussex. He also states that there had been some clothing trade here, but that it had been cut out by the introduction of hop growing at the end of the sixteenth century.

There are but few old buildings of interest in Farnham. In Downing Street is an early timber cottage with projecting front.

Close to the Jolly Farmer, Cobbett's birthplace, is a timber house, and an excellent bargeboard, of which I give an illustration.* The peculiarity is that a circumscribing line runs round every two quatrefoils. This is hardly discerned at first, but has the happy effect of taking off the monotony of such examples as those at Shamley Green. The timbers of the house appear to have been lately uncovered. They are plain uprights, and doubtless other houses with these bargeboards have similar timbers. There is a small carved bow-window opposite here, alluded to on page 39.

An old house opposite Castle Street has lately had its old timber-work reproduced. I give a sketch of old brackets from it. There is a corner house in Castle Street with some character, and there are some good specimens of Georgian work. I have given on page 46 some specimens of ironwork, and on page 51 drawings of the old Town Hall. The old ornamental front was taken down to widen the street, not many years ago, and the present plain wall erected. As the building is quite small, it is to be hoped that the people of Farnham will some day put up a front in character with the other work, and, if evidence exists, similar to the old.

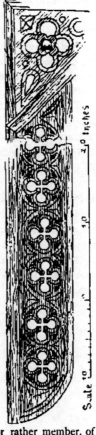

Farnham had originally a Corporation, the unreformed members, or rather member, of which got into trouble about a bridge, and surrendered it to the bishop in 1790.

There may possibly exist in this neighbourhood some examples of interest not drawn by me. I have not explored the country so thoroughly as in other directions,

* I am indebted to Messrs. Tompsett and Kingham for a rubbing of the tracery of this bargeboard.

9—2

as the buildings are scattered and the distances great.   I know, however, that there is nothing of importance.

Frensham Beale minor-house is old, and of some interest, and Chert is an old and out-of-the-way settlement.

There is an old place by the station at Tongham, and Poyle House is said to contain some Jacobean panelling.

Tilford was probably a rather important ford of the Wey, connected with Waverley Abbey.   A charter of King John refers to the King's Oak here.   A very fine and vigorous tree is generally pointed out as the identical tree, and is so figured and described by Brayley.   It is evident, however, that this could not be what was probably a noted tree at the time of the charter, and Cobbett mentions it in his ' Rural Rides' as 'a very small tree when I was a boy.'

Elstead is a little village on the road from Farnham to Godalming.   It is possible that the bridge called Somerset Bridge gets its name from the 'sumæresforda' mentioned as a boundary of Farnham in the charter of A.D. 909.

Near Seale, another small village on the slope of the Hog's Back, is Shoelands. This originally belonged to the priory of Selborne in Hants, but passed into the hands of the family of Lushers, one of whom, Sir Nicholas, built the present house in 1616, as a date on the porch tells.

There is an old hall inside, with its fixed seat and table, and the present tenant has many antiquities.   The fine staircase I have figured on page 16, and a chimney at the back is shown on page 29.

The chief feature outside is the large projecting porch with a room over it, that retains its old mullioned window of chalk.   The arch of the porch has been coated with cement.

AT COMPTON.

AT COMPTON.

PHOTO-LITHO, SPRAGUE & C° LONDON

COMPTON : COTTAGES.

Puttenham is a village on the slope of the Hog's Back, a recommendation of whose air and water has been noted by Aubrey, and has been handed down as a tradition ever since. There are some brick cottages of 1685, and I have drawn a later porch on page 22.

It is sometimes supposed that the house called Puttenham Priory occupies the site of a religious house. The name is, however, merely distinctive of that half of the manor that passed into the hands of the priory of Newark, in this county.

The name Puttenham has been conjectured to mean a village of wells, and has been compared to a cognate word in Belgium, but it is more likely derived from ' Putta,' a personal name often occurring in the charters.

Compton, together with Bookham, Effingham, the two Clandons, Albury and Henley, is mentioned in the earliest charter of Chertsey Abbey, A.D. 675,* as part of the lands granted to it, Frithenwald being subregulus of Surrey. Kemble marks this charter as of doubtful authenticity, but at any rate it is as old as a charter† of 787, by Offa, King of Mercia, confirming it. All these places, it will be seen, are on the Downs, beyond which, I conclude, settlement did not at that time extend.

I have already drawn the front of the upper cottage in this plate,‡ and remarked on the excellence and simplicity of this double-hipped form of roof. The management of the small roof to chimney, springing from the hip, should be noted. In this cottage the hipped roofs are continued down to cover pigsties, but that is, of course, a feature that could not now be adopted.

The other cottage is an early example. It has been considerably restored, and so well that it is not easy to distinguish between the new and old work. The framing seems old, but the chimney new. The corbelled corner-posts, in this instance, are cut out of solid butts. The door below is of chalk, and seems modern, but may be a reproduction of an old one.

* Cart. Sax. 39.   † Cart. Sax. 251.   ‡ See page 31.

COMPTON AND LITTLETON.

In the sixteenth century Compton passed into the hands of the Mores, who were leading people in Surrey. Sir William More built himself a large house of stone, with chalk dressings, at Loseley. One wing of this has been taken down, but the remainder is a fine and carefully preserved example of an Elizabethan house, and contains some fine carved chimney-pieces and ceilings. These are figured in Brayley's 'History of Surrey,' and the house is too important in character to come into the scope of this work.

Sir George More, the great man of the house, was a trusted supporter of King James whom he entertained at Loseley. He was Chancellor of the Order of the Garter and Lieutenant of the Tower, and was a very active man in county matters. He seems to have been a great builder, and having had to deal, in one way or another, with nearly all the estates in the neighbourhood, must have left his mark upon the art of architecture.

Loseley is noted for the celebrated collection of manuscripts preserved there, which are principally of this period.

Near this place are some rather extensive cave burrows, excavated in the sand-rock, that seem to have been lost sight of till some years ago. It has been suggested that they had something to do with the pilgrims, as the old way passes them. From their appearance it seems more likely that the sand has at some time been dug out for building, or for glass-making or some similar purpose. It has also been suggested that they were used by smugglers, which is quite possible.

Close to Loseley is the old manor-house of Littleton, renamed, probably in honour of William III., Orange Grove. The house is L shaped, and looks as if it might be interesting; it is too much covered over with ivy to be sketched. The cottage adjoins the house.

The farmhouse below is an example of a very typical old form. We have here, the central hall recessed, with the bracketed wall-plate, as described by Mr. Baily in the paper I have referred to. The way the two hips are treated is a curious form that I have seen elsewhere. The place has been very much done up, and I take the gablets over the windows to be modern additions.

AT LITTLETON.

AT COMPTON.

PHOTO-LITHO, SPRAGUE & C? LONDON.

AT BINSCOMBE.

AT BINSCOMBE.

BINSCOMBE.

Binscombe is a hamlet between Compton and Farncombe containing several nice cottages.

The upper of those shown is another example of the double-hipped parallelogram spoken of at Compton.

The lower cottage has a fine chimney-stack with crowsteps, which, however, are much damaged.

These cottages are partly built of rough Bargate stone with brick dressings. The wide joints of the rough stone are stuck over with small black ironstone pebbles, called 'galleting.' This is distinctly a Jacobean feature, and I think not to be found in older work.

FARNCOMBE AND UNSTED.

The little cottage at Farncombe is on the road to Binscombe, and of stone and brick, with a good chimney.

The house at Unsted I have mistakenly dubbed manor.   The old manor-house was on the estate now called Unsted Wood.

The name Unsted is an abbreviation of Tunhamstede.

In 1577 the estate passed from the Stoughtons to the Parvish family.   Henry Parvish, who died in 1593, describes himself in his will as citizen and haberdasher of London.   He was a considerable benefactor to Guildford.

In 1608 his son sold it to Sir George More, who passed it on to George Austen, one of another important landowning family at this period, who located themselves at Shalford.   By him it was sold in 1650 to the trustees of the Henry Smith who left so much money to the parishes of Surrey, and about whom, under the name of Dog-Smith, a ridiculous legend used to be current.   In the hands of the parish, as local trustees, the estate has continued since.   Another but less trust-worthy account says that the reversion was given by Henry Smith in his lifetime in 1627, and that he laid out £1,000 on the property.

It is an interesting house ; the large door, that now has a porch added to it, is arched, and similar to that at Alfold House, and the chimney occupies the same position relatively to what would have been the screen.

The windows are of unusual and quite Gothic detail, and the brackets are worked into the sills in the same manner as those in the house in High Street, Godalming.   The pattern of the framing on the first floor is also similar.

The chimneys are remarkably graceful.   I have given a measured drawing of them at page 23.   Of late years ivy has been allowed to grow all over them, so as to conceal their form.   It is to be feared that this most mischievous plant will have done serious damage, and it is to be hoped it may be cut down before the damage is irreparable, and be hereafter confined within reasonable limits.   One side of the roof retains the old Horsham slates.

AT FARNCOMBE.

UNSTEAD MANOR.

GODALMING.

Godalming is an interesting and flourishing little town.

In West-Saxon days the place was part of the royal possessions, and is mentioned in the will of King Alfred. It continued under the Crown until Henry II. granted the manor and the Hundred to the Bishopric of Salisbury, in exchange for two castles. That it had not been altogether out of the world, we may judge from the fact that at the time of Domesday the churches were in the hands of the famous Ranulf Flambard, afterwards the minister of William Rufus.

Attached to the Bishopric of Salisbury the manor remained until 1541, when it passed through the hands of Sir Thomas Paston into those of the king. It remained in the possession of the Crown till, in 1601, Elizabeth granted it to Sir George More.

The town seems to have been always busy and prosperous, as it furnished a notable contribution to the various Commissions of Array. It commanded, as it to some extent still does, an immense rural district, as there is no town between it and Petersfield and Midhurst, in the middle of Sussex; even they must have been to some extent contributory to its trade. Good water-power gave facilities for manufactures, and the extensive flat river meadows were in those days of value for grazing, although the floods are not of so fertilizing a character as in many parts. The name Salgasson shows that the meadow above the town is as old as Saxon times.

Godalming was early a manufacturing centre. The charter of Queen Elizabeth, A.D. 1575, quotes the inhabitants to the effect that the town has fallen into 'most extreme ruin and decay,' and that of James I., A.D. 1620, confirming this, recites that it is 'an ancient clothing town, and the inhabitants thereof of long time and before the memory of any man to the contrary have been principally employed in the making, dying, fulling, and dressing of woolen cloth.'

Probably the 'decay' was more or less of a rhetorical flourish, as towns in decay hardly seek incorporation, and other evidences point to the town's prosperity.

Aubrey says that there was here a manufacture of 'mixed and blue kersies for the Canaries, which for colour are not equalled by any in England.' He also says that 'whited brown paper' was first made in England, in Surrey and about Windsor. Also that there were grown here 'great quantities of liquorish and carrots, and great store of peat.' The two former were grown toward Shackleford.

Liquorice was, at one time, in immense vogue as an infallible specific for the liver, and carrots were grown for the manufacture of sugar.

The fulling mills at Westbrook are said to date from 1646.

There have always been, as there are still, a variety of manufactures carried on.

10

GODALMING: WHITE HART AND HIGH STREET.

The lower illustration is of the White Hart Inn, a most interesting example. My sketch was taken some years ago, and the lower story has been further modernized since. The original lower front stood two feet back from the first floor, as may be plainly seen at the gateway. This entrance was then only the height of the ground-floor, and has been raised since. It probably was similar to that shown on the other sketch. This is the inn at which Nicholas Nickleby is said to have put up on his road to Portsmouth, and it should therefore be dear to lovers of Dickens. In my time it has been several times threatened, and it is earnestly to be

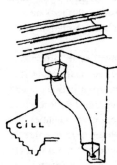

hoped that should it have to be dealt with, it will not be destroyed, but that a little judicious treatment in the way of jacking up and repairs, may preserve for several generations a building so interesting and such an ornament to the town; the illustration is of one of the corbels.

There were several considerable families resident at Godalming. The Westbrooks took their name from the small manor adjoining the railway station. Through an heiress their property came to Thomas Hull about 1549. He was one of a notable family in the neighbourhood which was settled at Hambledon.

The house shown in the upper sketch seems to have belonged either to him or the Westbrooks, since there was, till lately, in one of the back windows, a very good leaded coat-of-arms, of which I have a tracing. This agrees with the coat described by Manning as that of Westbrook.

'Quarterly, 1st and 4th, gules a leopard's head, jessant a fleur-de-lys; 2nd and 3rd, sable a fess indented between three fishes naiant: impaling argent a chevron gules between three mullets pierced sable, for Warner of Sheppey.'

This piece of glass is now in the possession of Ellis D. Gosling, Esq., of Busbridge. I mention it the more particularly as its existence is not chronicled in the county histories.

The plaster has recently been stripped off the further gable of this house, and new timbers inserted after the pattern of the old, but I am told there were more old timbers. The pattern of the framing is similar to that at Unsted,* the detail of the window-sills of which resembles that of this house, given on the cut above. Details of the bargeboards are given on page 36; as there mentioned, they resemble those at Nursecombe.† It will be seen that the original arched gateway to the back remains.

* See page 72.   † See page 79.

HIGH ST GODALMING.

THE WHITE HART, GODALMING

PHOTO·LITHO. SPRAGUE & Cº LONDON

HART LANE, GODALMING.

THE MINT, GODALMING.

Although the Manor of Westbrook passed to the Hulls, branches of the West-brook family long continued in Godalming. The manor afterwards came into the hands of the Oglethorpes, a Yorkshire family. It was a son of Sir Theophilus Oglethorpe who was said to have been introduced in a warming-pan, and have become the Old Pretender.

The narrative of Mrs. Frances Shafto, which had an immense vogue in its time, gives many curious details of her stay as one of the household at Westbrook, and of her sufferings and abduction in consequence of her becoming privy to the affair.

General Oglethorpe was a very distinguished man indeed, the founder of Georgia, and the mover in the reform of English prisons. He built the walls and tower, so conspicuous from the station, and planted the vineyard, out of which Bishop Pococke, in 1756, tells us 'they make a wine like Rhenish.'* The General also introduced edible snails and lizards ; he was a friend of Pope, Arbuthnot, and others, and there is an interesting history of him, written by Mr. Wright. The house looks very modern outside, but probably conceals much that is old.

GODALMING : HART LANE AND THE MINT.

There was a mint in Godalming in Saxon times, and there are extant a fair number of gold coins struck here.

This does not imply such a great importance as might be imagined, since, except in a very few instances, the Saxon mints were confined to places on the personal property of the king, and subject to his complete control.

This name, attached to a particular part of the town, is a remarkable instance of the survival of a name long after the origin of it had been forgotten.

A cottage close to the mint is shown in a cut on page 6. I fancy it was part of the Westbrook estate before the railway cut into it.

In coaching days, Godalming was of great importance as it was one of the stages on the road to Portsmouth. At one time the service was worked by Mr. Moon, the landlord of the King's Arms, who in 1816 arranged the journey of the allied Sovereigns on their road to Portsmouth. The King of Prussia and others lunched at the King's Arms, an immense inn, now partly a private house. The Great George was another large inn, now shrunk to corner premises, the remainder being given up to shops. The black and white marble pavement of the hall still remains in Mr. Jeffries' shop.

The smaller George has some very excellent cut brick columns and entablature of classic design.

* Dr. Pococke's 'Travels through England,' vol. ii., page 163.

10—2

Godalming : Church Street.

Another great Godalming family in Elizabethan times was that of the Elyots. They came originally from Green Place, Wonersh, but settled in Godalming in the reign of Henry VIII. One of the cadets, Laurence Eliot, obtained a grant of Busbridge. He is said by Manning to have been with Sir Francis Drake on his voyage round the world. I cannot find evidence of this, although it is on record that he was interested in the voyage. The probability is that, whether he went himself or no, he invested money in the undertaking, and it is to be supposed had a share in the £80,000 which was the result of the expedition. Probably, Eliot was brought in contact with Sir Francis at Esher Place, where one of the Drake family lived, and where the illustrious captive of the Armada, Don Pedro de Valdez, was afterwards quartered.

Busbridge Hall is modernized, but, I believe, contained old oak panelling in some of the rooms, that may have formed part of the original house.

Another and older branch of the Eliots settled in the house adjoining Godalming Church. This, though modernized externally, has a good deal of interesting work inside. The stairs are similar to those leading to the Warden's room at Abbot's Hospital, and the upstair rooms are panelled. In one room is a mantelpiece with three shields charged with the bearings of Eliot impaling successively Heneage for the grandmother, of Newdigate for the mother, and Berkely for the wife of George Eliot who lived here. His father, Thomas, of Tangley, died in 1623, so that will give an approximate date.

That part, at least, of the house was older is shown by the fact that what was probably the hall had linen-pattern panelling, some pieces of which are still preserved. A date over the porch, 1086, said to have been copied from a stone found in the cellar, has probably had an old-fashioned four or five mistaken for an ' o.'

The upper cottage in the plate has some panel partition upstairs. The other is of interest, as it probably was built for cottages, and is not part of a larger house perverted. It is mentioned in a deed of 1669, whereby Stephen Coston parts with his two messuages in Church Street.

On the opposite side of the street to the upper cottage, is one whose massive timbers seem to argue an earlier date than either of these.

CHURCH ST GODALMING.

CHURCH ST GODALMING.

WHARF ST GODALMING

OCKFORD ROAD, GODALMING

Godalming: Wharf Street and Ockford Road.

The cottages in Wharf Street are a pleasant group not improved by the slated lean-to. A long block of old cottages above them with a picturesquely twisted roof is, I hear, doomed, and will probably have disappeared before this book is issued. There is a crowstep chimney at the back.

The Waggon and Horses Inn, on the Ockford Road, stands quaintly some feet below the highroad on a steep slope. The long range of windows is a characteristic feature of old houses, which the need of repairs and the window-tax have seldom left unblocked. The lead lights have, within the last few years, been replaced by plain glass.

On page 47 and the following pages, I have given drawings of the two very fine brick houses in High Street. That of which I have given the measured front, belonged to, I imagine, and was probably built by, the Gore family, who were settled here. Sir Edward Turnour, Knight, created in 1661 Lord Chief Baron of the Court of Exchequer, married the daughter of Alderman Gore, of the City of London. From him are descended the Earls of Winterton, of Shillinglee, Sussex, who owned this house in 1755.

There is a nice timber-house overlooking what is called the Square, opposite the King's Arms, and the brick gable on page 51 occupies one side of the Square.

There was, some years back, a very quaint brick front opposite the Town Hall with a recessed brick porch. I have given a drawing of the door to it on page 40.

In Bridge Street formerly stood what was known as the hunting lodge, variously of King John, King Henry, and King Charles. A finely-carved panel, removed from here, and now in Mr. Stafford's museum of curiosities, is certainly of the last date. There is a confirmation of the tradition in an incidental statement in Mrs. Shafto's narrative, already referred to, that, on a certain day King William III. came down to Godalming hunting, and slighted the Oglethorpes by going to Mr. Bridger's to luncheon instead of to them. The hunting-ground was probably the park, which is said to have stretched over Munsted and Hyden's Ball to Burgate.

The lodge in Bridge Street was pulled down in this half-century, and stood next the old timber malthouse, which may have been connected with it. A few years ago a large quantity of oak panelling was taken out of a small house in Bridge Street, which was pulled down.

FARNCOMBE.

Farncombe was a hamlet on the opposite side of the river to Godalming, and consisted of a few houses and cottages scattered about the cross-roads. There are a good many nice old cottages left, though they are almost buried in the new town that has sprung up all round them. Probably workmen of the paper and woollen factories lived here in the seventeenth century, as they do now. Farncombe proper lies along the upper road where the church now stands, and the lower portion along the Guildford highroad is called Mead Row. The house now called Llanaway, from a false Welsh analogy, was called Lanaway in 1608, when the parish registers chronicle the burial of a suicide at Lanawaies Cross. Lanaway occurs as a personal name in 1619, and the place is called Lanway's Cross in Bowen's Map, 1749.

The two cottages shown are both of the double-hipped form, of which I have spoken. In the lower is seen the way the overhanging eaves of the roof were cut out over the windows, to allow the latter to open, and to give them more light. This is, of course, not feasible where gutters are used. The lower cottage has this year been cut up under repair.

In Mead Row is a nice old block of almshouses, founded in 1622 by Sir Richard Wyatt, citizen of London, and owner of Hall Place, Shackleford. It is now vested in the Carpenters' Company. The front is quite simple, but the back, which I have drawn at page 24, is picturesque. I have given a plan of one room on page 11.

In the centre is the chapel, which is unaltered and contains some quaint detail. An account of the place was published in vol. iii. of the Surrey Archæological Society's Transactions.

It is, perhaps, worth while re-chronicling that up to 1782 the entrance to Godalming was through the ford, by the side of the present bridge. The old bridge was only opened in times of flood.

A cave was discovered some years ago at Farncombe containing the bones of many animals; a description was published in the Philosophical Society's Transactions.

AT FARNCOMBE.

AT FARNCOMBE.

NURSECOMBE BRAMLEY.

NURSECOMBE BRAMLEY.

NURSECOMBE.

On what was the old direct road to Hascombe stands an interesting old house at Nursecombe.

Since my sketch was taken, many years ago, the house has been repaired. Some improvements have been effected in the windows, but the old bargeboard in front, which was similar to that still remaining at the back, has been replaced by a burlesque copy. The pattern of this was very similar, if not identical, to that on the house in High Street, Godalming. Some curious pendants remain to the wall-plates which I have figured on page 36. It is curious that there is a pendant to the top of the back bargeboard, but none to that of the front. The doorway has prettily carved spandrels to the four-centred arch. The form of porch is of the normal character, rather larger specimens of which are at Tangley and Burningfold.

I find I have, by a slip, spoilt the symmetry of the framing at the back ; both of the lower curved pieces should be in the corners.

A little higher up the road, on the opposite side, is an old house, at Snowdenham, above the mill-pond. The outside is covered up, but there are some door-posts of early date inside that might be fifteenth century.

There is also a stable, unusually complete, that must be quite early seventeenth century.

In the map by Senex, of 1729, as well as in Aubrey's map which is probably taken from it, this road to Hascombe is shown as coming from Guildford, through Bramley. No road is shown from Godalming until Bowen's map in 1749. The absence of a bridge at Godalming may have had something to do with this.

THORNCOMBE STREET.

At Thorncombe Street, on the same road, are one or two old cottages. Of one of these I give two views, as it is a particularly happy example of combinations of lean-to roofs. An interesting feature is the projection of the weather-tiling to form a hood, under the protection of which hung the gardening tools. Often one sees a ladder comfortably stowed away in a similar position, as shown in a sketch on page 12.

In this hamlet is an old farmhouse called Slades, which has a nice oak staircase of eighteenth-century date, and well-designed and carried out woodwork of the same date. The house had lately been in the hands of a careful tenant of the old school, and it was curious to see in the best rooms, the perfect condition of the papers and white paint, which had probably not been renewed for 100 years.

Further on this road is Hascombe, little more than a hamlet. Hascombe Hill overlooks the Weald, and is a landmark for miles. On its southern side is a Roman camp. The present road from Godalming is of modern date, and probably owes its origin to the development of Brighton, as the road is still called the Brighton Road, where it leaves Godalming. Hascombe Hill was originally a park, or enclosed place for deer. On its side is 'the lodge,' which was the technical name for the tenement pertaining to a park. Some way off, on the opposite side of the road, is Burgate, an old house which is famous for the fine Spanish chestnuts at the back. When the house was added to, some years ago, a secret chamber was found, formed by taking a piece out of one room. The access to it was from the garret, and it communicated with the cellars. From the discovery in it of some malt, it was conjectured that it was concerned with illicit distilling, rather than with the hiding of priests or others.

There is a nice old house at Hoe Farm that I might almost have given as an example. An interesting feature that existed a few years ago, and may still be there, was a cider-press fixed to the back wall.

Winkworth is an old timber farmhouse which has a brick porch of a pattern that seems to have been used freely on the Austen Estate, and that is not without character.

AT THORNCOMBE STREET.

AT THORNCOMBE STREET.

AT WONERSH.

GREAT TANGLEY MANOR.

GREAT TANGLEY AND WONERSH.

Returning northward, I next take Great Tangley Manor, which has the most showy front of any timber house in this division, and perhaps in all Surrey. A good description of this has been given in Mr. Baily's article, before referred to.* The front was added on to an older hall in 1582, as a date on one of the corbels tells us ; at the same time the old hall was divided into two stories, as I have previously stated was so often the case.

A magnificent tiebeam and king-post, with arched struts, remain in the room above. The tiebeam measures in the centre 1 foot 8 inches deep, by 10 inches wide. The windows are of rich and good detail, and the brackets are elaborately carved. The place of the screen to the hall remains, but the old work is supplanted by plain rounded posts which are certainly not original ; the rooms are panelled inside.

There was originally the usual wing beyond the hall on the side of the large gable, but it is probable that this was taken down at the time these alterations of 1582 were made, or perhaps by Lord Grantley, who did some clearing away at the beginning of the century. Tangley was acquired in 1542, through marriage, by Richard Caryl, a younger son of Sir John Caryl of Warnham in Sussex, a family of some importance.

He died in 1575, and in his will describes himself as citizen and mercer of London. This is an instance of the custom for cadets of good family to take to trade ; unfortunately, the will throws no light on his occupation of Tangley. There is, however, mention of his lease of the parsonage or rectory of Shalford, 'which I bought of George Elliotte, gent., which did cost me the sum of £960.' It must have been his son John, who died in 1612, who carried out the alterations. We find him largely concerned in dealings in land in the neighbourhood.

Tangley was, some years ago, in a very poor state, but it has happily fallen into kindly hands which have zealously preserved the old work. The ground has risen round the house, so that it is sunk about a foot below the proper level. There is a moat all round, and a walled garden with oval brick loophole openings of picturesque character.

The house above is the Grantley Arms, the sign of which I have carelessly omitted to show. The arched heads of the gable window, cut out of board, are peculiar.

* See page 14.

WONERSH.

Wonersh is a little village that, with others hereabouts, is said to have been formerly engaged in the manufacture of blue cloth for the Canaries. It is not likely that the demand, in the Canaries themselves, was large enough to keep this trade going, and it is probable that the island was used as a depôt by the Spaniards for goods to be sent to South America, the trade with which was jealously guarded.* The trade in blue stuffs is said by Aubrey to have been lost through the misconduct of the manufacturers, who found a mode of stretching the cloth beyond its natural length. It is certain that there are several Acts of Parliament dealing with this and similar malpractices.

The two cottages shown are in the street of the small village. The upper one has the characteristic recessed centre, of which mention has been made, but one side has been pulled down to enlarge the neighbour's garden.

The other cottage a little resembles that in Church Street, Godalming.

There are one or two other nice old cottages, and a very graceful single star chimney with some moulded brick in the head.† On the east of the village is an old timber building, and close by a very nice specimen of a square Queen Anne house with high hipped roof and sash windows. Close to it is a square cottage to the same design, rather like a doll's-house. There is an old frame house called Yieldhurst beyond the mill, rather complete, but perhaps near the end of its days. The mill-house is charmingly picturesque, and a fit subject for a painter.

The big house was till lately the seat of the Nortons, Lords Grantley, and is a good specimen of a Georgian house that seems grafted on to an older dwelling, or that at least preserves older traditions. It was, perhaps, built by the Richard Gwyn who owned it in 1701. There is a long gallery on the floor above the state rooms. The stairs are in a position indicating early date.

* The foundation of the trade was the very large import of wine from the Canaries and Teneriffe.

† See page 29.

AT WONERSH.

AT WONERSH.

AT BRAMLEY.

PLUNKS: SHAMLEY GREEN.

BRAMLEY AND PLUNKS.

Bramley was originally an important manor, and became split up into several members. The manor-house of Bramley East stands opposite the house shown at the top of the plate. It is a three-gabled brick and stone building of good proportions, and is illustrated in Brayley's History.

Most of the neighbouring manors were acquired by the Carylls, of Tangley, and were divided among the three daughters, coheiresses of John Caryll, who died in 1656. Mention is made of Bramley East and 'another house,' which is probably that shown.

From its similarity to the work of Tangley, this was no doubt the work of John Caryll; I imagine, however, that this porch-like building is an addition to an older house. This stands in a small court, so that it is impossible to obtain a true sketch of the work, and it has to be shown somewhat distorted.

Shamley Green is a little hamlet with a collection of old houses and cottages.

Plunks is an early house; the front is double-gabled, and no doubt there is good timber work behind the plaster face. The quatrefoil bargeboard is all plastered up and only visible in one place. This is similar to that shown on page 36, and on the same page is given a detail of the joist-board. It is evident from both of these that the house is at least quite early sixteenth century. The main front faces the east, so there is little doubt that the timber work would be found in good order, and it is to be hoped that the plaster will some day be taken off and the bargeboard picked out, when the look of the house will be much improved. The timbers will probably be straight, the house being older than the fashion for ornamental quartering.

At the back is a good example of the mode of forming and covering an oven at a later date.

SHAMLEY GREEN.

The house shown in the upper sketch I take to be, together with Plunks, older than most of my examples. I judge this from the carpentry of the gable top and cove, as well as from the traceried bargeboard and other signs.

The shape of the curved pieces is unusual here, but similar pieces are shown from Eden Bridge in Mr. Baily's article, and there is similar work at Mascalls, a very fine old timber house in Sussex. The bargeboard is shown on page 35.

This gable is in reality painfully distorted from the neglect to jack up the corner post when it was last repaired. I have in the sketch taken the liberty of restoring it to something nearer its true position. On the other side is one of the corbelled-out windows usual at the date.

The other house is a good specimen of what I take to be fairly early date. The framing of gable and the bargeboard are similar to those at Alfold House and an old cottage at Brook Green.

On the road to Wood Hill is a quaint group at Reel Hall, but, unfortunately, it had just been covered all over with new weather-tile when I saw it.

I have already given plans of two cottages on Blackheath. Adjoining, there is a nice long timber farmhouse at Halldish or Aveldersh, an old manor. There is also some old work at Northcote Farm.

Hull Hatch is also an old frame house.

AT SHAMLEY GREEN.

AT SHAMLEY GREEN.

AT CRANLEIGH.

FIELD PLACE, DUNSFOLD.

PHOTO-LITHO. SPRAGUE & C? LONDON.

CRANLEIGH AND . FIELD PLACE.

Cranleigh is a considerable village, notorious in old times for the badness of its roads, which lie on the clay. The village is somewhat modern, and does not contain much of interest.

The cottage shown may be usefully compared with others at Chiddingfold* and Dunsfold,† which are of similar outline. The artful way in which a gablet is formed to the near lean-to is worthy of notice. Two chimneys sadly want tall pots, when the outline would be very happy.

Not far from Cranleigh is a picturesquely situated farmhouse at Willinghurst.

I have nothing from Ewhurst, but Mr. Binscombe Gardner has published a drawing of Loseley Farm which shows a good example of coved weather-tiling, similar to that at Tuesley.‡

Near Cranleigh is Baynards, where Jane Roper, the daughter of Sir Thomas More, lived with her daughter, the wife of Sir Edward Bray the younger. Here she kept the head of her father, which was ultimately deposited in St. Dunstan's, at Canterbury.

Sir E. Bray sold the place in 1577 to Sir George More, who erected a dwelling-house, which he sold to the father of the famous John Evelyn, possibly when, in 1601, he came into Loseley. The old part is said to be incorporated in the large new house erected by the brother of Lord Chancellor Thurlow, but I have never been able to identify it. There were several curiosities preserved here, but the property has lately changed hands.

At Sansoms, inside a very commonplace brick front, is some old work. A corner of the room is panelled and seated, and the table stands in its original place.

Field Place, Dunsfold, I show as an example of picturesque tumbling-together of roofs. At the further end is a high brick and stone wing; apparently, the owner intended to rebuild the old house on a grander scale, and stopped short at this. This is one of the numerous small manors that abound about here; it anciently belonged to the Dean and Chapter of Windsor, who owned it in 1555.

* See page 59.   † See page 86.   ‡ See page 65.

DUNSFOLD AND BURNINGFOLD.

Dunsfold is a village of small houses and cottages, scattered round an extensive green.   Few of the buildings are later than the seventeenth century, and there are numbers of picturesque cottages ; the chimneys in particular are good.

Dunsfold Mill Farm is well shaped, and the little inn in an orchard, on an island, is an excellent specimen of an old place.   An interesting feature is the kennel for a dog formed near the entrance, I think under the oven attached to the large chimney.   There is a considerable timber farmhouse, called Willards, of irregular character.

The upper sketch is of a very nice little compact cottage that stands on the common near the entrance of a large new house.   It is to be feared that it will be destroyed, though it is in very good preservation.   In the angle is an unglazed window with wooden stanchions and shutter, such as I have described at Black-heath, page 12.

Somewhere by the church, what is known as Sussex or Petworth marble used to be dug, in the memory of man, and the road leading from the church to the well at the river edge is composed of the disintegrated shells.   In all the old houses and cottages, steps and paving-stones made of this are to be found, and in the better houses it is used for mantelpieces.

The parish is on the clay and is mainly agricultural, though it may have supplied workers for glass or iron works in Chiddingfold or other parts.

The name Dunsfold may come from the personal names Dunna or Dunne, which are found rather frequently in the Saxon charters and in this part of England, or it may come from ' Dun,' an eminence.

The house at Burningfold is one of the best in the district, and the front shown is in good preservation.   It lacks, however, the rich detail of Tangley.

The room under the verandah has lost its old window, but retains good panelling inside.   The name is thought to come from ironworks that once existed here, in which case they must have been of great antiquity, as the name is old.   Close by is Furnace-Bridge.

DUNSFOLD COMMON.

BURNINGFOLD.

AT ALFOLD.

AT ALFOLD.

PHOTO LITHO. SPRAGUE & Co LONDON.

ALFOLD.

Alfold is the most primitive village in this part of Surrey ; it lies on the very border of the county, in the middle of the clay-lands, and, until the turnpike road was made, away from any important highroad.   Even till lately the access to it by any but the main road was almost impossible in bad weather.   The cottages about here remained in a very primitive condition, and old ironwork, such as fire-backs and dogs, candle and rushlight stands, etc., might be readily obtained.   Something yet remains, but the best of it has been collected.

The name Alfold, Awfold, or Aldfold, is generally thought to mean Oldfold, but this must not be taken for granted.   The prefix 'Al,' as is proved by the Saxon charters,* is sometimes a contraction, as Æthelwoldington, near Peterborough, has become Alwalton.   'Al' in Alton, or Aulton, in Hants, is not, as has been assumed, the old town, but the town on the 'Awel,' the name of the river,† or, as Kemble says, of the headsprings of a river.   Carshalton is doubtless from the same root.

In this neighbourhood are many sites of old houses and manors, but the buildings have generally either been pulled down or improved out of archæological or artistic interest.   A not infrequent survival is the moat, a feature of easy manufacture in this clay soil.   Many of these are of mediæval date only, but some seem to belong to far earlier times.

The old buildings in this country are generally roofed with Horsham slate, which was procured close at hand, but was also carried much farther into the country.

The cottages shown are, I find from a recent visit, practically things of the past. The top one is re-roofed with common slates, and the other has been enlarged and improved out of all character.   The village was a charmingly rural one, but the breath of the pestilence has passed over and vulgarized it.

The little cottage shown on page 9 has been pulled down altogether.   It had corbelled-out windows and other early features.   It stood opposite the green, and when sketched was used as a school.

* Birch, Cart. Sax., No. 909.   † No. 390.

ALFOLD HOUSE, AND COTTAGE.

When I first sketched Alfold House, nearly twenty years ago, it was in an interesting state, and I regret now that I did not take further particulars. The wing with the arched door was empty, and used only for storage.

A peculiarity was that the whitewash had peeled off the fine oak beams, and showed that they were covered with distemper patterns of arabesque character of rude but contemporary date. The rough ledge door to the bedroom, over the hall, was covered with a strong flower pattern, boldly sketched in with a broad, black line. This was the most complete instance I have seen of the little value attached by our forefathers to the natural surface of oak. Had the house been inhabited, the distemper paint would, probably, have long been scrubbed off.

The windows are now a good deal altered. The plan I have given and discussed at page 14.

The framing and bargeboard follow those described at Shamley Green and Brook.*

The two parts of the cottage above are not at right angles, but set askew. The chimney is an unusual form, each flue projecting 4½ inches beyond the other. There is a similar chimney on the farmhouse at Alford Park, and I have met with it in some other places.

At Tickner's Heath, Cobden's Farm has an old interior with some fittings.

Rickhurst is a largish farmhouse, one room of which is in very perfect, original, and picturesque condition. It has the fixed bench along one side, and the long table *in situ*.

In the large wood near here, called Sidney Wood from a mediæval proprietor, some glassworks were started by French refugees, after the Revocation of the Edict of Nantes; in the churchyard are the memorials to some of them.

In the fourteenth century Alfold came into the hands of the Butlers of Ormond, of whom I have spoken under the heading of Shiere.

* See pages 84 and 64.

AT ALFOLD.

ALFOLD HOUSE.

AT ALBURY.

PHOTO-LITHO SPRAGUE & CO LONDON

SHOPHOUSE FARM, FARLEY.

Albury and Shophouse Farm.

In the wild country from the borders of Sussex to the Tillingbourn Valley are many isolated places, but none of great interest.

There are old cottages at Madgehole, Jelleys, and Colman's Hollow. The latter name, which occurs elsewhere in similar places, may commemorate Colman, the king's huntsman. Mayor House Farm is an old place of splendid colour but rude shape. St. Mary Holmbury is a new settlement, but there are a few unimportant old cottages at Felday, as there are at Peaslake, where is a fairly quaint building that was a Quaker's burying house. Hound House has some old work at the back.

Hoe Farm is a timber house, rudely framed with great curved struts, and has to me a look as if it might be of unusual age. Such framing is often shown in manuscripts.

Sutton, near Felday, is a pretty settlement with a number of excellent cottages of quite plain form ; good examples of how little show is required for the picturesque.

There is a farmhouse of no particular interest, and the site of an important house that was pulled down about the beginning of the century. A cottage that stands near what seems to have been the site of this house may have been part of, or connected with it. There is a corbelled-out window upstairs of solid make.

Wolven's Farm has a brick front of some character.

Shophouse Farm and the cottage at Albury have little more of interest than their roofs. On Farley Heath stood a Romano-British town. It is said that as late as 1639 the ground pinning of the buildings stood as high as the banks, but were in 1670 removed for building or road material.

The name Albury, spelt in Saxon charters Eldeberrie, really does mean Oldbury. This place, with the Clandons, Compton, and the county north, is enumerated in the grant made to Chertsey Abbey in A.D. 675.

There is not much of interest here. An important house, called Weston House, was pulled down many years ago, and a fine Spanish mahogany staircase from it is now in the County Club at Guildford.

GOMSHALL AND ABINGER.

The farmhouse at Abinger Hatch has no business in this collection, as it is outside the division; I drew it and Paddington Manor, on the succeeding plate, inadvertently. They are, however, so near to Shiere that they practically belong to it more than to Dorking. I regret that I had not, at the same time, drawn an extremely interesting house at Abinger Crossways. This, however, must be left as a plum for some other work. This Abinger Hatch farm is another good example of the beauty of a plain roof. It has also a fine stone boundary wall. There is no form of fence that, for appearance, can touch an old stone wall laid in mortar. The varied tints, and the curious mosses and plants that grow on it, give it a nobility that nothing else can equal. The chimney is the best example about here of the panelled form.

Gomshall was the ancient manor embracing all this part of the country. If the theory of late Saxon settlement be correct, Gomshall was probably the manor created by the Mercian kings at a time when the country was wood and waste. As the country became more settled, the manor was broken up into many others of more manageable size.

The house is a very good specimen, but such repairs as have been made have not been very judiciously done. The pattern-work is smeared over with plaster, and does not actually show as clearly as it does in my drawing.

There is a very fine block of chimneys, a detail of which is shown on page 24.

There are no notices extant as to the history of this house, and I am unable to make out whether it was a manor-house, but it seems to be connected with the Tower Hill Estate, from the mansion of which it is now cut off by the railway. There is another house at the corner of the road, called the Ivy House, which has old work. The Rev. I. R. Dummelow, curate of Shiere, tells me that there is here a legendary staircase, and large carved chalk mantelpieces.

Tower Hill, one of the manor-houses of divided Gomshall, has some panelling and armorial bearings on a ceiling. Its name is derived from St. Mary Tower Hill, London, to which it belonged. Netley is named after its former possessor, the abbey of Netley in Hampshire; the farmhouse is said to be old.

AT GOMSHALL.

NEAR ABINGER HAMMER.

SHERE.

Shere is a village of importance and antiquity. In mediæval times it was part of the extensive possessions of the Butlers, Earls of Ormond, who had their capital mansion and favourite English residence at 'la Vacherie,' or Vachery. Several of the family lived a great deal here, and were buried in, or were benefactors to, the fine church. Few family annals contain a roll of such distinguished men.

From the Butlers the property passed to the noble family of Audley. There is a half-brass in the church to John Touchet, Lord Audley, Lord High Treasurer of England.

It is worth noting, as an illustration of the intestine strife in England, that Shere Vachery belonged to the Butlers, strong adherents of the House of Lancaster, while the other half of the divided manor, Shere Eboracum, was the property of the House of York.

Vachery was probably in mediæval times the most important place in the neighbourhood, since of all the important families, who owned estates, that of the Butlers seems to have been the only one that was constantly resident. At one time Philippa, Queen of Edward III., was a visitor at Vachery. The mansion has long been pulled down, and only a farmhouse and the moat of the mansion remain.

The property next came to Sir Reginald Bray, the famous minister of Henry VII., and in the family of his nephew it remained, and in part still remains.

The ownership by such important families, residing on the place, doubtless gave an impetus to Shere, and accounts for its having a rather more architectural character than usual. Aubrey says there was here a very ancient manufacture of fustian, and that accounts for the number of cottages. There is a legend that the old parsonage house, that stood near the stream, was built upon wool-sacks. It has been conjectured that this was a figurative expression, in connection with which I may mention that there was an old ballad, or, rather, dance tune, called 'The Building of London Bridge upon Wool-sacks.'* The bridge is said to have been built by a tax on wool. It is just possible, however, that the foundations of both may have been laid on wool-sacks filled with concrete, just as the Thames banks are mended to this day.

* The London Chanticleers, Scene VIII., Dodsley.

Shere and Paddington.

There are many excellent bits of work in Shere, but few subjects for a general sketch. The cottage shown has a detached star chimney of unusual size. The square of it must measure over 3 feet externally.

Bargeboads are shown on page 35, and a joistboard, page 36, from a very old cottage in Lower Street. This cottage has the recessed centre and corbelled-out wings typical of early work, and is probably fifteenth century.

Paddington Manor, as I have said, is outside the division. It is an old house with a richly-carved bargeboard, similar to those of Shamley Green. The whole front is covered with rough cast; as it faces north, it is certain that the timbers are in good condition, and it is a pity that they are not exposed to view. The house is charmingly situated, and well worth such a little attention, though one must not expect more than plain uprights. The manor belonged to the Leighs of Stockwell from 1489 to 1543, and in 1549 went to the Brays; perhaps it dates from that time, but I take this class of house to be nearer the beginning of the century.

A survey of the manor taken in 1557 returns thirty messuages, ten cottages and ten tofts, which gives an idea of the buildings existing at the time.

There is an interest attaching to this manor that has not yet been pointed out, namely, its connection with a hero of romance.

Manning and Bray record that, in 1305, it belonged to Adam de Gurdon, but they miss the signification of this proprietorship.

Most people are, I suppose, acquainted with the ballad and the story of the bold and gigantic outlaw, Adam de Gurdon, and how Prince Edward encountered him in the woods, and vanquished him in single combat. The fight actually took place in a wooded valley between Farnham and Alton, and Prince Edward brought his prisoner to Guildford and presented him to his mother, who was holding Court there. He was pardoned and restored to his estates, or, at least, granted some estate, and there can be no doubt that this Adam de Gurdon, holding Padingdene in the 33rd of Edward I., is the man.

AT SHIERE.

PADDINGTON MANOR.

PHOTO-LITHO. SPRAGUE & Cº LONDON.

CHILWORTH.

Chilworth is a hamlet at the foot of St. Martha's. There were early powder-mills here, and Elizabeth, anxious to render the country independent of Germany, whence the best supplies had been drawn, imported workmen, and settled them here under Sir Polycarp Wharton, who was granted a patent for the purpose. Like most inventors who serve Government, Sir Polycarp was badly treated, and allowed to end his days in prison, because the Board of Ordnance could not find time to settle his grievances. In the last few years a fresh importation of a German process has taken place, and a large establishment is at work on an improved gunpowder for heavy guns.

There was a cell, belonging to the priory of Newark, where Chilworth Manor now stands, and the large walled and terraced gardens of the monks remain, as well as their stew-ponds for fish. It is supposed that the monks attended to the services at St. Martha's, which was a salient point on the Pilgrims' Way. The old manor-house of Chilworth has an ornamental brick gable and porch.

On the other side of St. Martha's is the farmhouse called Tyting, in the kitchen of which is a group of three early English lancet windows of chalk.

SHALFORD.

Shalford is another village of houses scattered about a green and along the high-road.   Probably it was a favourite country retreat from Guildford, as there are a number of houses of some pretension.   These contain various remains of old work, though they are not interesting externally.

Near the mill is a very good house which has its back to the road.   One gable is of stone, with very ornamental brick dressings, and this and the other gables resemble the other work that I have described and illustrated in the chapter on 'Brick and Stone Buildings.'   Apparently the owner had began to reconstruct the house, but had stopped short.   I cannot find anything of the history of the house,

except that it is shown on an early seventeenth-century map of the Austen Estate, as then existing with three gables.   As Shalford House is shown, at the same time, as quite a small house, I think possibly this mill-house was built by the Austen family before they moved to Shalford House.   The family of Duncombe had also a house in Shalford in the seventeenth century.

The house illustrated on this page has a fine and rather unusual staircase, of which I give a drawing.   What is equivalent to the balustrade is cut out of solid planks.   The rustication of the newels is a feature also to be found at Slyfields Manor-house.

There is a good door-head, and the house is panelled almost throughout. A few years ago it was divided into two poor cottages, and all the panelling was battened over and concealed from view. Since then it has been most judiciously and conservatively renovated, and is a most interesting example.

Shalford House itself, the seat of the Austen family, possesses one panelled room with a carved mantelpiece. This is well drawn in Brayley's 'History of Surrey.' It has the interesting motto carved on it, 'Hyeme incalesco æstate refrigero'—a proof that our ancestors were sufficiently alive to the advantages of open fireplaces.

On the other side of the river, near St. Catherine's, is a picturesque old cottage with some circle work, but it has always struck me as being a very good imitation or reconstruction, and not original.

In the meadows, at the approach to Guildford by the Shalford road, is a picturesque block of cottages, but they are so much out of repair that I fear they must some day go. The houses on this side of the road have

a good deal of character, since on one side they open to the road, and on the other drop suddenly—at least, a story.

GUILDFORD: FARNHAM ROAD AND CASTLE ARCH.

I cannot attempt here to give any general account of Guildford, which is also the less necessary as, besides the larger histories, very fair guide-books exist. I shall only therefore exhibit the sketches and give an account of the architectural features.

My first sketch is of a block of houses close to the station. These are covered with rough cast, and only noteworthy as forming a picturesque group. They have the reverse feature to that I have noted in Quarry Street, in that the hill rises sharply behind them, and their doors have to be approached by flights of steps.

The other cottage is built on to the walls of the old castle-gate house in Quarry Street.

Inside are interesting chalk mantelpieces in the Jacobean style, and there is a fine external door. This work, no doubt, dates from the period when the castle was granted by James I. to Francis Carter, who turned it into a residence.

There is an old door to a cottage in Quarry Street near the entrance to the caves.

Within the last few years, the castle and its grounds have been acquired by the Corporation, and they are now accessible to the public as a garden. King Henry III. was a constant resident and a considerable builder here, and there are rather full records of his doings.

Although rather out of my scope, I will here allude to the two mediæval crypts in High Street. One is under the Angel, and has been recently cleared and fitted up as a saloon, so that it can be seen without difficulty. There is no connection at all between the two, but they are very similar in style, and I have sometimes thought they might be the undercrofts of a gate-house that may have closed the road, in connection with the town or the outer precincts of the castle. Such gateways as I mean remain at Canterbury and Lincoln.

FARNHAM ROAD, GUILDFORD.

CASTLE ARCH.

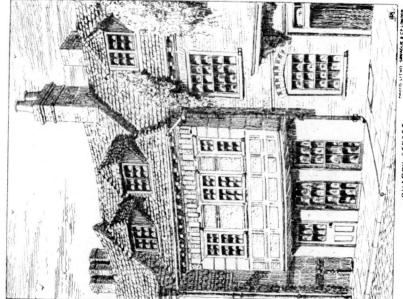

QUARRY STREET.

WOODBRIDGE ROAD, GUILDFORD

Guildford : Woodbridge Road and Quarry Street.

The house in the Woodbridge Road is, as far as I know, the only one in the district of a form usual in many parts, and especially in stone countries. The roof is formed by a succession of gables which begin a short distance from the end and are separated by only a short interval. The ridge is level with that of the main roof, and as the gables are narrower than the main roof, their springing is consequently above that of the other. I have seen ranges of five or six such gables in other places.

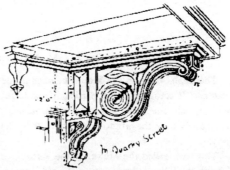

The Quarry Street house has an old timber front that has been coated at later date with ornamental plastering. The cornice is similar to others in the town that I shall speak of later. This house, as well as the others along this road, drops very much on the other side.

When the Virginian creeper, next door, is in perfection, this whole corner is a splendid piece of colour.

There is a capital hood to the doorway of the adjoining house, but it is toppling to its fall. It is to be hoped that so good a piece of work will be properly secured before too far gone.

Nearly opposite here in a modern-looking shop is a black-letter inscription on a beam. The house is said to have been for the priest of St. Mary's.

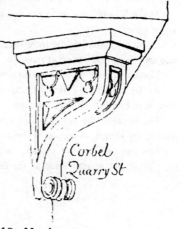

I give a corbel from a corner house in this street. The projection is 1 foot 6 inches, the height 2 feet.

GUILDFORD: ON THE MOUNT AND IN THE MEADOWS.

The small house on the Mount belongs properly to the section of ' Brick Architecture.' It seems to me a particularly graceful little design. The depth of the panels is only one inch, as to which I have made some remarks on page 50. The little panels over the windows are filled with flint and would, perhaps, be as well away.

This part, called the Mount, is the starting of the old Farnham road that goes right up the hill, on the course of the old Roman road, which is very visible about a mile further on. It is a very charming bit of street, and contains some good houses.

At the bottom, adjoining the bridge, is a very fine old house of the Christopher Wren style.

In Bury Fields, leading from here, are some pieces of Jacobean wood-work built into a cottage, and drawn at page 50.

There is a door with a very interesting carved head a little further on.

At the corner of Friary Street, on the other side of the bridge, there is also a very large and fine Georgian house.

The house in the Mead is that familiar from the railway, and looks better thence than in my sketch, which lacks the good colour of the original.

The fine brick house in Leapale Road I have illustrated on page 52, and also the picturesque garden-house at the foot of Ward Street.

ON THE MOUNT, GUILDFORD.

IN THE MEADOWS.

PHOTO-LITHO, SPRAGUE & CO LONDON.

56 & 57 HIGH ST

PHOTO-LITHO, SPRAGUE & CO. LONDON.

48 HIGH ST, GUILDFORD.

GUILDFORD : HIGH STREET, NOS. 48 AND 56.

The High Street of Guildford is, undoubtedly, one of the most picturesque in England. It starts from an old stone bridge over the Wey; not many years ago there was from the bridge a charming view of the tower of St. Mary's Church and the keep of the Castle. Such a view ought to have been worth a good deal to a town that owes a large measure of its prosperity to its residential attractions. Unfortunately a new block of shops has been erected, that shuts it out.

The High Street ascends a steep hill, and the houses are continuous for the greater part of the way. They are nearly all built of timber, and mostly date from the period of which I have been chiefly treating. They have, however, been re-fronted in all styles ; in many cases high fronts conceal low roofs, and what seem to be substantial brick walls are really nothing but what is called 'mathematical tiles,' fastened to the old timber fronts. Those not used to this form of imitation brick will be much puzzled with the apparently inexplicable jointing, and with the manner in which seemingly solid brick walls are supported on almost nothing.

There is an astonishing variety of overhanging bow-windows, which are chiefly of late seventeenth-century date. On a cursory glance one might set these down as merely picturesque, but a closer inspection will show that, for delicacy of detail and accuracy of proportion, they are worthy of close study, and, perhaps, are as likely to be useful to the architect as the more early and more archeologically interesting timber buildings. They seem to me particularly valuable as models for terra-cotta work.

The shop-fronts have necessarily been modernized, but, happily, the upper stories have remained unspoilt, to the credit of the townsmen, who have been proud of what is undoubtedly the greatest attraction of their town, and have not, to any great extent, exchanged their good old lamps for vulgar new.

Near the top of the High Street stands the Town Hall, a building that has been constantly illustrated of late years, and whose projecting clock and other features are therefore familiar. This was erected in A.D. 1685, and it is evident that to the same designer and workmen we owe many of the bow-windows and cornices in the High Street. The window of No. 48 is the best of several of similar design, and is evidently inspired by the Town Hall. The windows of Nos. 56 and 57 are of an older form : the lead lights have been replaced by sashes, and the curious circular bow above is, no

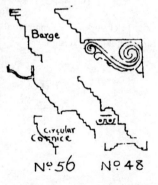

doubt, an addition. It is not unpicturesque, though hardly to be imitated without considerable modification.

GUILDFORD: HIGH STREET, NOS. 18, 30, AND 31.

Nos. 30 and 31 are of later, I suppose of Georgian, date and are good examples of classic work. In these and some of the other windows the detail is very elegant, as is usually the case when classic detail is carried out on a sufficiently small scale ; it is only in cases of exaggerated size that the effect is tedious and wearisome. Looking at such examples as these, it is easy to understand how the style obtained its hold on the building world.

I should mention that the casings and mouldings in these, as well as nearly all the other examples, are of deal.

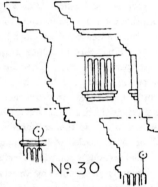

Nº 30

Next to this house is a Bank, till lately one of the old-fashioned private country banks. It has one of the most graceful classic fronts to the lower story that I know of anywhere—a model of design. The inner frame of the windows has been modernized, and some carved fanlights have had to give way to the necessity for more light. The date must, I should say, be at least fifty years earlier than 1834, that appears on the front as the foundation-date of the late Bank. The front of this, as of most of the other apparently brick houses, is of the tiles I have spoken of.

Nº 31

No. 18 has a cemented front, probably applied to older brickwork. Its ornamental features are much later : I give it for the sake of a certain quality of design.

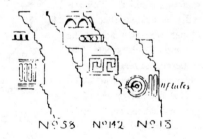

Nº 53   Nº 142   Nº 13

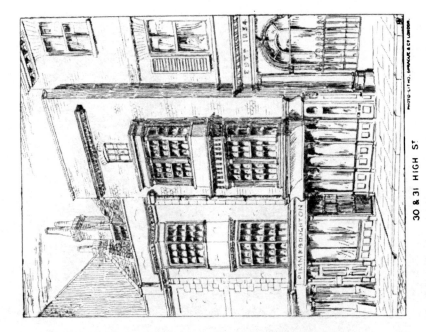

30 & 31 HIGH ST

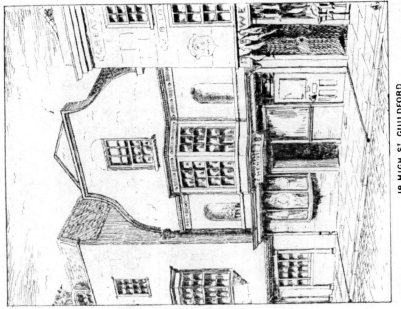

18 HIGH ST, GUILDFORD

GARDEN FRONT Nº 25

PHOTO-LITHO. SPRAGUE & CO LONDON.

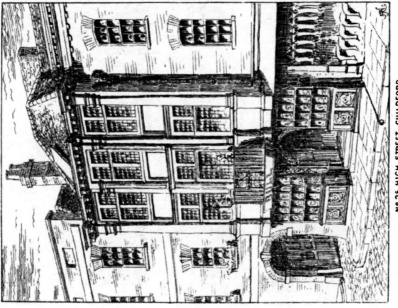

Nº 25 HIGH STREET, GUILDFORD.

GUILDFORD : HIGH STREET, No. 25.

No. 25 was a very fine house erected by the Martyr family, who were hereditary town clerks of Guildford. The room on the first floor in front has a fine plaster ceiling, and there is a good ceiling to the bow-windowed room at the back. This front room is always appropriated, at Assize times, to the High Sheriffs. There is also a very fine carved oak staircase, the panels of which are of similar style to the carving on the bow-window at the back, and the panels fitted under the shop fronts. The front door is a very fine piece of Christopher Wren style. A great glory of the house is the fine ironwork of the casements ; some of these I have shown on page 44.

As far as I can make out, the classic timber front is a casing put up to the original house to which the windows belong. The sash windows shown in an annex at the back seem to belong to this latter date, rather than do the lead lights and iron casements. Of the same date seems the door at the back and the flight of steps, the wing walls of which are a little clumsy.

The windows at the back are good examples of the bold and deliberate use of the square section frame ; this wall also is covered with tiles.

A little above this house stands the hospital built by Archbishop Abbot in the reign of James I. Besides a general propriety of design, this building has the advantage of having been very little tampered with, and possesses a series of splendid oak doors and a very fine staircase to the Warden's rooms. There is other interesting detail in various parts, and the old benches and tables remain in the common room.

It has also a remarkably fine set of chimneys of excellent design. No one visiting the hospital should omit to go into the garden, where is a fine flight of steps and good view of the building. I do not know of much remaining inside the houses at Guildford, but it is probable that quantities of panelling and other work may be concealed behind battening.

A few years ago I purchased, from a house that stood where the new London and County Bank now stands, a room full of panelling and a carved Jacobean mantel ; this is now at Ote Hall, a house I have already alluded to.

I may here mention that there is in the Council Chamber, at the Town Hall, an excellent stone mantelpiece delicately carved with figure subjects. This was brought from Stoughton Manor at the time of its demolition.

GUILDFORD: HIGH STREET, NOS. 140 AND 133.

In Spital Street, a continuation of the High Street, is the old Grammar School, that has a stone front dated 1550. There is a good Jacobean door with a head similar to that at the White Hart, shown on page 41. A smaller door is cut out of the large door.

The old schoolroom, with its old fittings, remains in this building, but is, I believe, to be shortly cleared out, to suit the arrangements of the new organization.

At the top of the High Street, on the south side, opposite Abbot's Hospital, stands Trinity Church. This has a central flight of steps and iron gates and railing that form altogether a splendid bit of design of which any town might be proud.

In Chertsey Street is a repetition of one of these gates. There is also a fine iron gate to Stoke House.

The White Hart is an old house with very modern front; I have given some details from the back. Another inn, the Angel, preserves its large panelled hall and staircase, with painted canvas frieze and clock. There are some remains of the old Jacobean entrance under the gateway; something has been done to these since I first wrote, but still more might, I think, be made of them. A few years ago there were some curious long curved struts to a projecting building at the back; these had a scroll carved on the ends. They were displaced by recent improvements, but a pair have been fitted to the carriage-way. Visitors should not omit to see the thirteenth-century vaulted undercrofts of this house, now fitted up as a saloon.

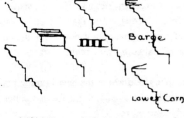

N°140   N°141   N°134

The White Lion is also a very old house, but I do not know of any old work in sight.

Nos. 141 and 140 have old windows to which, as well as I can make out, classic block cornices have been fitted, at some time after the building of the Town Hall. The same remark applies to No. 133 and No. 134, an older house, to which, perhaps, bow-windows have first been added, and afterwards cornices.

133 & 134 HIGH ST

140 & 141 HIGH ST, GUILDFORD

121 HIGH ST.

125 HIGH ST, GUILDFORD.

GUILDFORD: HIGH STREET, NOS. 125 AND 121.

A feature of the High Street is the continuous character of the houses. Doorways between them lead into the little narrow courts characteristic of old towns. At the entrance to one, adjoining No. 124, is a Tudor arch still remaining.

No. 125 is another instance of ornament applied to an older house. I had always supposed that the original roof was hipped, and that the top of the gable had been added. Since my sketch was made, the upper part has been carefully repaired, and I find that this is not the case. The artist who added the blocked cornice must, therefore, have the credit of its happy arrangement. Thanks to this recent repair, I am able to give the accurate detail of the upper cornice, which supplies a key to that of the others, which are only sketched.

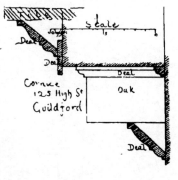

The blocked cornices of Nos. 125, 134, and 140 are similar, with a trifling difference in the lower members. The blocks are of oak, but the mouldings of deal, cut, as will be seen, from very thin stuff, and slightly nailed up ; the lower member is not closed in at the top.

No. 121 is of an earlier type, that, taken with the brick pilaster at the sides, suggests the school of Inigo Jones.

Lower down, at the corner of Quarry Street, is an old house with a number of gables of picturesque outline, but so stuccoed over as to be hardly worth giving.

Various old buildings of importance have vanished from Guildford. On the site of the old Friary an important Elizabethan house was built, with a front of alternate squares of chalk and brick. This belonged to various noble families.

Brabœuf Manor, at St. Catherine's, had, perhaps, the finest timber front in the neighbourhood ; it was only taken down this century, and is shown in some existing drawings. An old view of Guildford also shows an important Jacobean house in the Bury Fields. Possibly the door-posts, illustrated on page 42, may have come from here.

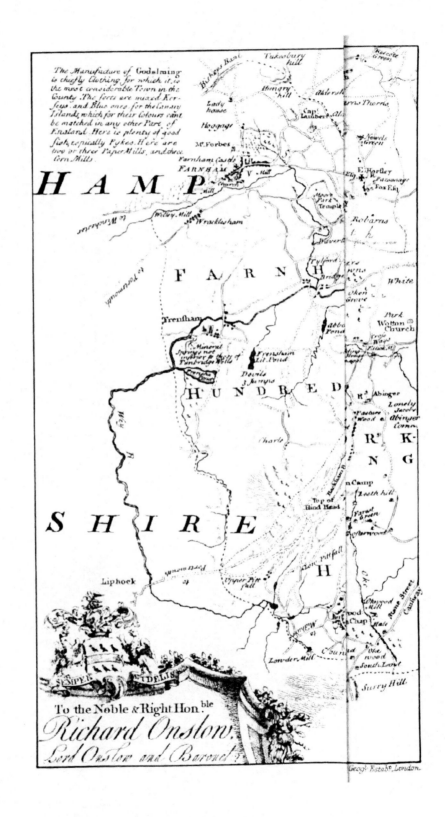

The Manufacture of Godalming is chiefly Clothing, for which it is the most considerable Town in the County. The sorts are mixed Kerseys, and Blue ones for the Canary Islands which for their Colours cant be matched in any other Part of England. Here is plenty of good fish, especially Pykes. Here are two or three Paper Mills, and three Corn Mills.

H A M P

F A R N H

H U N D R E D

S H I R E

SEMPER FIDELIS

To the Noble & Right Hon.ble
Richard Onslow,
Lord Onslow and Baronet

Geogl Establt London.

PART III.

ROMAN AND OTHER EARLY SETTLEMENTS IN
SOUTH-WEST SURREY,

AND THE

MARCH OF AULUS PLAUTIUS AND
VESPASIAN.

CHAPTER XI.

I HAVE explained, in the Preface, that the following chapters have really nothing to do with the purpose of my book. They are added as likely to be of interest to those living in the neighbourhood, and because it may easily happen that I may not again have the opportunity or the time to put on record what I have picked up during some twenty-five years of archæological study of the county.

I have hopes that, at any rate, these gleanings may prompt and help some other student to carry the work further.

Of the earliest inhabitants of these parts we have no certain knowledge. The writer of a very able article in the *Saturday Review*, a few years back, advanced the proposition that all this part of Surrey, with the valleys of the Wey and the Mole and the forest of the Weald, remained in the possession of the Romanized Britons till a late period in Saxon history ; he even thinks he recognises a different ethnological type in the natives.

He holds that the heath and forest land, on the borders of Hampshire, was the eastern boundary of the West Saxons, and that this part of Surrey, mostly forest land, ran up like a wedge between them and the kingdom of Kent. We have historical evidence of the existence of such wedges of British territory at Malmesbury and elsewhere ; the British forest kingdom of Elmet in Yorkshire, for instance, long maintained its independence, though surrounded by Teutonic invaders.

Mr. Grant Allen[1] has pointed out much the same fact, and states that he recognises a Celtic type in the population of the Weald.

Certainly the physique is very different from that of the Kentish people or the Saxons of Yorkshire, and certainly the foundation of the place-names is what we are accustomed to call Celtic. It may be open to question, however, whether the same causes that preserved the Romano-Briton from the Saxon may not also have favoured the survival of the old long-headed Iberian stock who built the long

---

[1] *English Illustrated Magazine*, No. 63, December, 1888.

barrows, of the broad-headed Finnish stock whose remains are found in the round barrows, of the Celts of the Welsh branch, of the Belgæ who succeeded them, and of the Frisians and other Teutonic tribes who seem to have been imported into this part of England during the Roman occupation. It is now generally admitted that there are survivals in England of all these races, and it therefore becomes important to be as accurate as possible in one's references to race.

Although there are numerous barrows scattered about the heaths, they have not been sufficiently explored to throw much light on the subject. It would be a most useful work, if what has been already done were tabulated and brought together, and further systematic and methodical exploration undertaken.

Those barrows which have been opened appear often to have been previously rifled, and have yielded no important results. In 1790 the Rev. James Douglas opened a tumulus at Gostrode, in the parish of Chiddingfold, and found a skeleton and a few other remains.[1] The very name by which the tumulus went locally, 'Golden Hoard,' was sufficient evidence that exploration came too late. Again, the name Gold Hill, belonging to a pyramidal hill at Chert, suggests the plunderer. This hill, by-the-bye, adjoins Kettlebury, a name that would seem of Saxon origin, since it probably commemorates the Thurketil, Ulfketil, Usketill, or one of the numerous names having this termination. There is also a 'Kettle the Huntsman' mentioned in Domesday, as a proprietor in Surrey. There is at present nothing to show whether these tumuli belong to the Belgæ, the Celts, or the older round-headed Finnish people. Certain it is that any early immigrants who may have landed in this island, in the county of Kent, must have passed along this road on their way into the interior.

The names of the rivers, such as the Wey, the Mole or Emly, and the Oke or Ock, are, as usual, Celtic, or such as we are accustomed to call Celtic. There is, I believe, in reality nothing to show that they are not survivals of an older language. Hill names are also constantly British ; an authenticated instance worth mentioning, since it has not hitherto been recorded, is that of Crooksbury, the well-known hill above Waverley. In a Saxon charter[2] relating to Somersetshire, we find the sentence 'juxta collem qui dicitur britannica lingua Cructan apud nos Crycbeorh.' This is also an interesting instance of the Saxon habit of tacking their own termination on to a British root—a practice the possibility of which has been disputed. The old suggested derivation from ' crux ' may be dismissed. Nennius[3] mentions among the marvels of Ireland, that ' Est ibi mons qui cognominatur Crucmare et est sepulchrum in cacumine montis.' The marvel was that the grave adjusted itself to anyone

---

[1] ' Nenia Brit.,' p. 162.   [2] Cart. Sax., No. 62, A.D. 682.
[3] Cap. cxxxvii.

lying down in it, whether he were long or short. On our Crooksbury is a tumulus called 'Soldiers' Ring,' where bronze implements were found.[1] In Owen's Welsh Dictionary of 1793, 'crug' is said to mean a barrow, and it is stated further that 'on such round hillocks the Britons held their bardic and judicial gorsezau, or assemblies; hence crug and gorsez are sometimes used as synonimous terms.' This not only fully explains the meaning of Crooksbury, but also that of Gostrode, where, as I have stated on page 107, the Rev. J. Douglas opened a tumulus. An older form of this name is Gorsted, and the form Gosterwood, that appears in other places, is a modern gloss.

Ockley perhaps owes its name to the river Oke that flows here, rather than to the oak-tree, as Bede[2] asserts; Saxon etymologies of this period are always to be looked on with the gravest suspicion. About Ockley, the steep ravines cut by the streams in the clay go by the name of 'gills.' This is a well-known name in Westmoreland and Cumberland—parts of the old Welsh kingdom of Strathclyde.

Some time before the period of Cæsar's invasion, all these parts of England had passed into the possession of Belgic tribes who had crossed over from France and Belgium, bringing the names of their settlements with them.

The late Mr. H. Lawes Long, of Hampton Lodge, in this division, has dealt very learnedly with the question in his 'Survey of the Early Geography of Western Europe,'[3] a work that deserves to be better known. Dr. Guest has also discussed the matter in his 'Origines Celticæ,' etc., and Mr. Elton in 'Origins of English History.'

These Belgic tribes were the Loegrians, who are carefully distinguished in the Welsh annals from the older Celts. Some writers have concluded, from the account given by Cæsar, that the Belgæ were Teutonic; but both Dr. Guest and Mr. Long show very strong reasons for putting them down as Celtic.

They were undoubtedly different from the previous Celtic population; probably in the same manner that the typical Gauls of France, who are thought to be identical with these Belgæ, are different from the Armoricans of Brittany, who are supposed to be akin to the Welsh Celts. It should be borne in mind, however, that Mr. Coote,[4] whose great work has so revolutionized the reading of our early history, maintains stoutly that the Belgæ were Teutonic or Low-German. He gives some excellent reasons, and certainly, if the fact could be proved, it would remove many difficulties. The researches of Mr. Seebohm[5] to some extent strengthen Mr. Coote's argument. Perhaps the alternative suggested by Mr. Seebohm may be found to reconcile the two views, and it may be that the race and language of the inhabitants of southern and other parts of Britain were profoundly modified, if not changed, by

[1] 6-in. Ordnance Survey.　　　[2] 'Quasi in campulo quercus.'　　　[3] Published 1859.
[4] 'Romans in Britain.'　　　[5] 'English Village Communities.'

importations of Frisian and other tribes,[1] made in the long period of 300 years, during which the Romans occupied the island. In any case, however, it is not probable that there was any extermination of the race of such peasants as those whose dwellings in Cranbourne Chace have been so thoroughly explored and commemorated by General Pitt Rivers.

As an example of the manner in which one race may remain unchanged in certain positions, although surrounded by another nationality, Mr. Long instances the Walloons of Belgium, a distinctly Celtic stock inhabiting certain districts of the Ardennes ; to this day they preserve language and other distinctive peculiarities.

Dr. Guest says that 'all Surrey south of the Hogsback may have been Welsh territory.' It will be worth inquiry whether, as the preservation of the word 'gills' seems to imply, the older Celtic population may not have survived in these forest fastnesses, after the occupation of the general country by the Belgic tribes.

If this were so, their refuges would be in the clayey lands intersected by numerous streams, since it was the water rather than the trees that rendered a forest impenetrable. On that question, however, I shall have more to say when speaking of the Roman occupation.

That the sandhills and chalk downs of this division were immensely inhabited in the earliest times, we may conclude from the enormous number of flint implements that are perpetually being discovered, sown almost broadcast over the country. A fine collection of these is in the museum of Charterhouse School, a great part of which were collected about the Hogsback by the Rev. C. F. Kerry, during his tenancy of a curacy at Elstead. Mr. F. Lasham, of Guildford, has also a fine collection, and Colonel Godwin-Austen has exhibited to the Anthropological Society some finds from Bramley. As a matter of fact, anyone who sets himself to collect diligently, from one end of the county to the other, may acquire a large collection in a few years. This must not be taken as peculiar to this district, since it is the case all over England ; still, for some reasons given below, there are grounds for thinking that this particular tract formed in early times a great highway.

That the Belgic tribes were settled here, we know from the finding of numerous gold coins of their kings, both at the town of Farley Heath and widely throughout the district. The late Mr. Whitbourn, of Godalming, had an extraordinary collection, chiefly acquired from finds in the neighbourhood, for acquiring which he had special advantages. Some are illustrated in the Surrey Archæological Collection, vols. i. and ii. If, as I have stated above, there remained in the forests on the clay an older race, it is likely that to the Belgic tribes we should attribute the large irregular camps that are found in the district, which do not correspond with what we know of

[1] See also Kemble, 'Saxons in England.'

Roman or Saxon or Danish work. The account of Vespasian's campaign shows that the Belgæ occupied such camps. Many curious moated places remaining in the clay countries may, on the other hand, be the fortresses of the older people.

Manning and Bray state in their preface to Surrey that the county was settled by the Segontiaci and Regni, whose original boundary on the west was the river Itchen in Hampshire. They also say that on the arrival of fresh immigrants in Hampshire, these tribes retired to the main body in Surrey. This is stated on the authority of Camden and of Baxter.

Baxter, writing in 1733,[1] says that the Segontiaci, whom he considers the same as the Regni or Rhemi, were a Belgic people who were originally settled in South Hampshire, but being driven out by a more recent colony of the same people, afterwards settled along the sea-coasts of Sussex as far as Kent. I am unable to find any possible source for this statement, but conclude it comes from Camden's identification of Ringwood or Rencewood,[2] as it is called in Domesday, with the Regni or Rhenci. The statement is very probably correct, but the Segontiaci were settled in North Hampshire, where they had their town Silchester or Caer Segont; this Mr. Napper is probably right in calling Ardaoneon,[3] the final part of which survives in Onion's Hole and Onion's Pennies, mentioned by Camden. About fifty years before the advent of Cæsar, a great part of Britain was under the rule of Divitiacus, King of Soissons, and it has been surmised that a colony had been planted by him in the island. The Belgæ proper were settled in Wiltshire and Hampshire, so that if fresh settlers of a colony had arrived from Gaul through Portsmouth or Southampton, it is very likely that they would have pushed their predecessors from Ringwood and those parts into Sussex. There is also a camp called Ringwood a short way from Southampton. I have noticed this matter, since anything stated by Manning and Bray is worthy attention, and Baxter was a man of genuine learning who may have had some further ground for his statement.

There is some further evidence of such migration that may be of value; this is the remarkable duplication of names in parts of Sussex, Surrey, and Hampshire. This is, I think, too significant to be considered only as accidental, and may also have prompted Baxter's statement.

Whether this nomenclature is to be considered as Belgic or Saxon is a difficult question to decide. The original names are certainly not distinctively Saxon; on

[1] Baxter, 'Glossarium Antiquitatum Britannicarum,' A.D. 1733. Voce Segontiaci : 'Hi cum fuerint ut et reliqui Britanniæ Primæ populi origine Belgæ a recentiore tamen ejusdem Coloniâ ad maris litora propulsi, Ptolemæi ævo a Regno sie Noviomago et Durotrigum finibus ad Mantantonem et Cantii fines omnem maritimam oram obtinebant : australis tamen Antoniana initio illis pro Patria fuerat.'   [2] Cart. Sax., No 650, Runcwudu, A.D. 925.

[3] It certainly is not Calleva, which was doubtless at Reading.

the other hand, they might belong to the Jutes, who were settled in the parts of Hampshire chiefly concerned. Even if the original names are British, as they certainly are in part, it does not follow that they were not transported by Saxon migrants. As the particular group of names that concerns this part of Surrey acquired, in Surrey, Saxon affixes, I shall speak of them under the head of the Saxon occupation, but without committing myself to an opinion as to which period they belong to. Both explanations can, in the absence of further evidence, only be looked upon as useful working hypotheses.

From the very earliest periods the track along these hills now represented by the Pilgrims' Way, must have been the highway of communication from the West of England to the Straits of Dover ; and if, as Mr. Elton considers, the tin of Cornwall was brought by the Britons to the Isle of Thanet for easy shipment to Gaul, it must have been along this road. Whether this were so or no, there can be little doubt but that this route, along the Hogsback and the Merrow Downs, was of the greatest importance as a long straight track of open country. I give a rough map on p. 119. Probably Cæsar's camp at Aldershot and the camp at Holmbury are two that served to guard the occupation of the road. From Farnham the road passed to Basing, and branched in one direction along the Downs past the camps of Winklebury, Burghclere, Walbury, and Chisbury to Marlborough. Another ancient road called the Harrow Way[1] runs from Basing, past Andover and Weyhill to Amesbury. It is to be noted that Basing is called in a charter of A.D. 688 Basingahearh.[2] This road must have been of the more importance as it led to Stonehenge, which there is little doubt was the central place of worship for the Belgic tribes of Druidical religion, just as Cæsar tells us Carnutium, now Chartres, was in France.

Even if the latest writer on Stonehenge, Mr. Arthur Evans,[3] who speaks with unusual authority, be correct in ascribing the erection of the stones to much earlier times, it does not follow that it was not used at this period as a sacred spot. Indeed, if, as he surmises, a sacred oak stood in the centre of the enclosure, that points still more to Druidism, which we know originated in Britain. Although the Saxons certainly did not use the same religion, they may well have given the name to a road to so important a sacred place, or they may have had a 'harrow' of their own where the famous Abbey of Amesbury afterwards rose. The road, at least, must date from the earliest period.

From Farnham a branch road passes through Alton to Winchester and Southampton, whence in later days streams of pilgrims passed along this track on their way to Canterbury. The church at Worting on the Harrow Way is one of the few dedicated to St. Thomas à Becket ; this looks as if pilgrims passed that way also.

---

[1] *I e.*, Sanctuary Way.   [2] Cart. Sax., No. 62.   [3] *Archeo. Review*, January, 1889.

CHAPTER XII.

THE ROMANS AND THE CAMPAIGN OF AULUS PLAUTIUS AND VESPASIAN.

THE advent of the Romans has left its mark on this part, as on every other part, of England. The principal work of theirs remaining is the Stane Street that runs from Chichester or Regnum to Dorking, and so to London. It has been sometimes suggested that this road was of late construction, made towards the end of the Roman occupation, and to connect with London the castles erected on the Saxon shore. One argument in favour of this is the silence as to so important a road in the Itinerary of Antoninus. It is sufficient answer to this objection to recall the fact that this Regnum had been under a friendly native king, and that there were no military precautions necessary.

In favour of the early date of the road it is to be noted that a pig of lead, marked as of the reign of Claudius, was found at Pulborough, a station on the road in the middle of Sussex. Now, though coins are no certain indication of earliness of date, it is at least unlikely that a pig of lead should remain unused for a couple of centuries and then find its way to such a position ; also, the undoubtedly Roman camp at Hardham, through the centre of which the road passes, does not look like a late feature.

That this part of Surrey was not always so peaceably settled is shown by the chain of castles or camps that are found about it.

It is generally safe to conclude that those of a rectangular shape are of Roman origin, and in that case we have an undoubted Roman camp on Hascombe Hill, as well as possibly one at Hillborough, adjoining Hampton Lodge.

There is, moreover, a name, common enough, that bears significant testimony to a Roman origin. This is the name Nore or Nower. Mr. Puttock, of Epsom, pointed out in the *Gentleman's Magazine*[1] that this name was the direct descendant from the Latin *noverca*, a mother-in-law. This was a term used by Hyginus and other Roman writers on castrametation for any point threatening or commanding a camp. Thus at Hascombe we have Nore or Nower, a farm on an adjacent height,

[1] *Gentleman's Magazine*, Reprint, 'Roman Remains,' vol. ii., p. 490.

and there is Nower at Bury Hill, Dorking. There is also a Nore or Nower at Shalford,[1] and the name is plentiful throughout England. Another form of the same word is Nork, as at Nork House, Epsom.

On Farley Heath, near Albury, are the remains of a Romano-British camp or town that was partly explored by Mr. Martin Tupper in 1848. Some elegant little tripods of enamelled work, the size of salt-cellars, were found together with Roman and British coins, and many other things. These may now be seen in the British Museum. Aubrey in his history, dated 1719, but composed 1676, records that in his time the foundations and base of a circular building were to be seen,[2] and there is little doubt but that this was a temple. Some explorations at the very similar station at Hillborough have yielded nothing, though I cannot but think there must be something there. On the heath adjoining Mr. Kerry found many remains.

A Roman villa was uncovered some years ago at Albury on Sir Thomas Farrar's property, and was the scene of interesting experiments on the work of earthworms by the great Darwin.

It has long been a favourite idea with those who have treated of the Roman occupation that the Wealds of Surrey and Sussex, part of the great forest of Andred, were impenetrable and that they were avoided by the Romans, who carried their roads by a circuitous route round the Hampshire skirts of the forest. This superstition has been mainly founded on a very doubtful interpretation of the Itinerary of Antoninus, and on a passage in an early chronicle which says that Andred was a dark and dangerous place, full of thieves and robbers.

Now, it is very obvious that a forest country, inhabited by a sturdy and independent race, would present great difficulties to a people who afterwards proved themselves so insignificant as the South Saxons. We have indeed a record[3] that, during the siege of Anderida, the miners of Andred came out and greatly harassed the attacking force under Ælla. I cannot but wonder that a passage so obviously one-sided as that mentioned above should ever have been seriously cited as evidence.

Had any record come down to us from the British side, it would doubtless, and correctly enough, have described the Downs and the parts beyond as an impregnable and inaccessible country, inhabited by sanguinary and ferocious pirates.

A good deal of misapprehension has also arisen from the confusion in our minds between the forests of tropical countries and those which we read of in early England.

As a matter of fact, the term 'forest' implied a wild unenclosed tract, but did not necessarily imply a continuous wood. No doubt this district was originally thickly wooded, but, after all, there is nothing very serious in the impediments to traffic in

M. and B., i. 652.   [2] See also p. 98.   [3] Hen. of Huntingdon.

an oak wood such as this was.   Brambles in the woods and furze on the heaths are the most serious vegetable growths, and can hardly be supposed to have stopped the Roman legionary; moreover, these only occur in the clearings.

As a matter of fact, the real impediments are the rivers and their valleys, and the small streams swollen to torrents in the winter months.   Anyone familiar with the localities knows how the flat meadow-lands of the Arun and the Ouse, subject to constant flooding, almost completely cut the Downs off from the interior.

In the summer the clay lands are dry and perfectly easy to traverse, but anyone who has hunted in the district knows what they become in winter.   This applies, however, chiefly to the belt of clay lying along the border, since the greater part of Sussex is occupied by the sandy forest ridge, which is easy of passage.   Of course, also, a forest tract in the hands of an enemy is a very different affair to an open country.

As a matter of fact, a very little acquaintance with local history is sufficient to show that the Forest of Andred was penetrated in all directions by the Romans, who had iron-mines in many parts, of great importance.

Though Andred was well served by roads in numerous places in Roman times, it is undoubtedly true that in later times, owing to the weakness of the South Saxons, and their failure to master the inhabitants, it became a sort of no man's land and refuge for outlaws.

I have attempted to show that a Roman road led due north, out of Chichester, by Cocking Causeway,[1] to Midhurst.   Midhurst has been identified with the Roman town of Mida, or Miba (the right version of the name is doubtful).   There seems, however, no ground at all for the suggestion beyond a certain resemblance of sound. Dr. Stukely,[2] however, says that the road here 'appeared to them to be Roman,' and Roman remains have been found near Cocking.

Leaving Midhurst, the road passes over Henley Hill, and where it descends the very steep hill there is still a very fine piece of paved road that is locally known as the Roman road.   I see no reason to doubt but that it is the original road, since it corresponds to the paving that used to exist on the Stane Street and in other undoubted positions.   I mention it here particularly, as it does not seem to have been noticed in any of the histories of Sussex.   The old highroad to Chichester went up this bit of hill, but in the early part of the century a more easy ascent was obtained by making a detour of about a mile.

This road, if continued, would reach Haslemere, and if carried thence in a straight line would pass over Hindhead, by Thursley, Elstead, and Hillborough, to Tongham, where most extensive Roman remains have been found, as narrated by Stukely.[3]

---

[1] Causeway, or Causey; from *calceata*, Latin for a made way.—Guest, i. 349.

[2] Iter vii.   [3] *Ibid.*

He says that 'innumerable coins, urns, and antiquities are dug up everywhere in the hedgerows,' and that 'many pillars, pilasters, capitals, bases, marble tables, etc.,' are dug up there continually. Many of these, he states, were in the possession of George Woodroff, Esq., of Poyle, late owner of the estate, who had 'many pecks of coins found there.'

There are reasons for thinking Haslemere to be an ancient settlement, and I have been informed [1] that some years ago, in digging into the highway, the surface of an old road was come to at a depth of 5 feet. The tradition recorded by Aubrey is that the old town stood south of the present, that wells have been found there, and that it was destroyed by the Danes.

From Henley Hill a road seems to have struck across in a direct line by the end of Black Down, on the extreme point of which is marked on the Ordnance map the suggestive name Castle Copse. This straight line continued passes the Roman camp at Hascombe, and finishes in the town at Farley Heath. If continued, it would reach London on one side and Portchester on the other.

In the parish of Chiddingfold on this exact route is a long, wide, green road, running along the crest of a ridge, and called High Street Green. High Street is a well-known name for a Roman road in such a position, the best known instance of which is the High Street that runs over the tops of the mountains in Westmoreland.

I pointed out some years ago the probability of this being the course of a Roman road, and my conjecture has received considerable support from what I learn from the Rev. T. S. Cooper of the mediæval history of this place. This I will not here anticipate, as it will appear in his history of the parish. I may add that this road is much more apparent when one stands on it than on the map.

Close to this road is the site of the Roman villa discovered a few years ago, some particulars of which were communicated by me to the Society of Antiquaries. The barrow at Gostrode, previously alluded to,[2] also lies on this line.

Another road has been traced by Mr. Park Harrison[3] leading from the Stane Street at Rowhook, on the borders of Sussex, to Farley Heath, and probably from thence to Guildford. I am told [4] that the paving of this road is still very perfect in some of the wooded 'rews'[5] at Coxland.

Another road to which I have called attention is that on the Hogsback, leading from Farnham to Guildford. A great part of this has been converted into modern highway; but where the old turnpike stood, a broad green road begins and runs to

---

[1] By C. G. Roberts, Esq.   [2] Page 107.   [3] 'Surrey Archæol. Transac.,' vol. vi.
[4] By James Sadler, Esq., of Cherfold.
[5] The word 'rew,' for a long hedge-like copse, from 10 to 20 feet wide, is an interesting survival of a word very common in the Saxon charters. As far as I know, it is peculiar to the Weald of Sussex.

Guildford. In the centre of this is a raised road and small ditch and bank each side, and I take this to be the original Roman way. The road is 16 feet across, the ditch about 10 feet each side, and 2 feet deep, and the bank varies. Dr. Pococke, in his travels in 1750, mentions the splendid road from Guildford to Farnham,[1] and the existence of a Roman road from Guildford to Ripley and doubtless thence to London. His evidence is always particularly valuable, as his travels were chiefly before the Highway Acts had destroyed the old roads. North of the Hogsback a villa has been found at Broad Street. A road or trackway called the Drove Road[2] from Guildford continued along the crest of the Merrow Downs to Dorking.

Mr. G. T. Clark, in his paper on Guildford Castle, has remarked on the singular absence of evidences of antiquity on these hills, on a soil that is chalk and therefore so retentive of any form artificially given to it. The fact, however, is that, along these Merrow Downs, the chalk is overlaid by a thick stratum of gravel, which is of course particularly unretentive.

Along the valley between the chalk and the sandhills are remains of Roman villas and other signs of occupation, from east to west of the county.

The discovery of the Roman villa at Chiddingfold was interesting, as it was the first, and is still the only one, found on the south side of the sandhills, and in what may be called the Weald. As no year passes without the discovery in England of several Roman villas, it is probable that numerous remains still lurk beneath the soil.

On the west of the county, in addition to the treasure found in White's time in Wolmer Pond, an immense find of over thirty thousand Roman coins has been made near Wolmer, and Mr. H. F. Napper has located there the Clausentum of Antoninus, as he has at Ewshot in Crondall the site of Venta Belgarum. This is too great a controversy for me to touch on ; but I may point out that his conjecture as to Ewshot as a place of settlement receives some corroboration from a passage in Dr. Pococke's 'Travels.'[3]

Certainly there was here an extensive Roman settlement. A villa has been discovered at Crondall,[4] and at Barley Pound, near Bentley, are earthworks, which are thought to be the remains of an amphitheatre.[5]

In a hopground at Bentley extensive remains of all kinds of pottery are constantly dug up. At Chert, on the desolate heaths, in this same district, there was, till a few years ago, a manufactory of rough earthenware. The jugs and vessels

---

[1] Dr. Pococke's ' Travels through England,' vol. ii., p. 164, and p. 169.

[2] I have been told that in my informant's boyhood droves of ponies were brought this way to avoid the turnpikes ; possibly they came along the Harrow Way from Weyhill horse-fair.

[3] Page 162.   [4] ' Archæologia,' xxxii., p. 54.   [5] 6-in. Ordnance map.

made here have been of the same shape from time immemorial, and are just what the Romano-Britons made ; certainly they are infinitely superior in form to modern work. On Bowen's map of 1749, Red Urn Green is marked at Chert ; modern maps have improved this into Redhearn and Redburn, but taking the existence of this pottery into consideration, I see no reason to doubt the correctness of the earlier version. Though Chert is now out of the world, it was in Roman times near the settlement at Wolmer, and those at Bentley and Crondall, and I am certainly disposed to believe that the pottery had existed there undisturbed from the time of the Romans. The manufacture is now carried on at Elstead, and the vessels may be bought in Guildford and Godalming. In the same way I should not be surprised to find that the glass-making that existed in Chiddingfold in the thirteenth century had remained there from the Roman times.

Some writers have held that the iron forges, so active in Roman days, were extinguished after their departure and did not revive till the fifteenth century. There is, however, no reason to suppose that they ever ceased working. Charter 73, Cart. Sax., A.D. 689, records the grant by Oswyn of Kent of the iron-mine at Lyminge in Kent. No. 594, A.D. 900, records the 'grundeliesan pytt' at Hurstbourne in Hants.[1] This I take to be 'iron ore pit,' but I offer this only as a conjecture.

It is not likely that such lovers and such users of iron as the Saxons, would suffer such an industry to perish, nor that patriotism would prevent the dwellers in Andred from doing a good business.

There are some other camps in the neighbourhood : a large one on Holmbury Hill, of which I have already spoken, and a very perfect one at Anstiebury, on the other side of Leith Hill.

In a paper read to the Surrey Archæological Society in 1888 on the famous battle of Ockley, A.D. 896, I dealt with these camps.

Anstiebury I take to be a late work, made probably by the Mercians on their taking possession of this country, or more probably by the West Saxons who succeeded them. Its purpose was to guard the important Stane Street which ran at its feet. In either case it was no doubt in connection with the castle at Ockley, where so many Witenagemots were held, and of which I traced the site adjoining the church as described by Aubrey.

Holmbury, from some peculiarities of parish boundaries, I was then inclined to think might be the Mercian headquarters before Anstiebury was made. Perhaps it may have been a Belgic camp, made use of by the Mercians before the incursions of the Danes had shown the vital importance of a closer defence of the road.

Mr. H. F. Napper, who has devoted much attention to these matters, tells me

---

[1] My memory is that this is elsewhere called 'grundeleisen,' but I cannot find the reference.

there is a small square camp at Shrubbs at the exit of the tunnel where the Guild-ford and Horsham railway enters Sussex.   He also reports on hearsay that there is another near Chert, but I have not been able to identify this.

I have already spoken of the three camps at Farley Heath, Hillborough, and Hascombe as probably Roman, and the question arises at what period they were made and used.

In A.D. 43 Aulus Plautius was sent by the Emperor Claudius to invade Britain. He landed in three detachments in three places, probably on the coast of Kent. An account of his campaign is given by Dion Cassius, and Dr. Guest has given a valuable paper on it.[1]   I was gratified to find that my own conclusions, formed independently, were confirmed by those of this great authority.

A letter on the subject from Sir George Airy, printed in 1860 in the *Athenæum*, No. 1683, is of no local interest.   It endeavours to show that Plautius landed in Essex, which is clearly untenable.

The difficulty felt by Sir George, as by others, is in understanding why the Romans should land in Kent, when it was well known that the headquarters of the enemy were in Essex.   This is, however, I think, answered by what I have said below of the influence of Bericus on the campaign.

Dr. Guest concludes that Plautius marched from Kent along the country on the south side of the Thames, and after fighting two battles, reached Gloucestershire, where he made peace with its inhabitants, the Dobuni.

Leaving Gloucestershire, the Romans forced the passage of the Thames, probably at Wallingford, and marched towards what afterwards became London.

If we may accept this as correct, the question arises as to the road taken by the Romans.   Dr. Guest suggests 'possibly along the Marlborough Downs.'   I think there can be little doubt but that the advance was made along the well-known trackway now known as the Pilgrims' Way.   There was certainly at this time no passage of the Medway at Rochester, but the ford was probably at Aylesford, where centuries later the invading Saxons had their great fight.

From this point the old road follows the line of hills through Ightham, where is the large British fortress of Oldbury.   In the invaluable new 'Archæological Survey of Kent,' Mr. Payne states his belief that the Romans, at some time not stated, made their way along here, attacking, and, as is proved by remains, occupying the older *oppida*, or hill fortresses.   The way then passes along the ridge north of Westerham into Surrey.   Its course has been traced through Titsey Park, where a Roman villa has been discovered, and by War Coppice[2] to Merstham.   Thence it passes Dorking, Shiere, Albury, St. Martha's, the ferry at St. Catherine's, and along

[1] 'Origines Celticæ,' etc., vol. ii., p. 394.   [2] Sir G. G. Scott, 'Surrey Arch. Soc.,' vol. vi.

under the Hogsback to Farnham. What is known now as the Pilgrims' Way is in places only a footpath, but the old track was probably of large extent, occupying hilltops as well as sides; Gatton and Walton Downs were on the high ground.

South of this track was the forest, and the impassable clays cut up by countless streams. On the north were the difficult valleys of the Mole and the Wey, and large tracks of boggy heath and swampy marsh.

Dr. Guest computes the army under Plautius as consisting of not less than 50,000 men—no inconsiderable force. We must remember, also, that the army was not wandering altogether in the dark, since they were doubtless guided by Bericus, a refugee of royal blood, who had indeed instigated the campaign. Cæsar's invasion

was by this time little more than a memory, but doubtless the natives would take care to carefully guard the road he took, and in especial Halliford, the place at which he crossed the Thames. Perhaps the camp on St. George's Hill was made after his invasion, to protect this ford. As Plautius would be sure to be informed of this, it is the more likely that he would have arranged another line of advance. If he did not intend to force the passage of the Thames at the same place as Cæsar did, there is hardly any alternative than the route I am supposing. The sketch-map that I give will show the impediments caused by the rivers, and especially the swampy and thickly wooded valleys of the Kennet and Loddon.[1]

[1] The Pilgrims' Way passes through the valley at Shiere and Albury, close to Farley, and not on the ridge, as shown in the map.

From the Hogsback the track either passes by Cæsar's Camp at Aldershot, and by Odiham to Basing, or, as seems more likely to me, through Farnham, past the Roman Works at Barley Pound Crondall, over White Hill, and by South Warnborough into Hayley Lane, and by Andwell, where the five lanes meet, and so by Hatch Lane to Basing. From Basing the road passes the large camp at Winklebury on Rook's Down,[1] then runs along the ridge south of Sherbourne St. John by Pit Lane to Woodgarston. This is marked in the Ordnance map as a Roman fort, and contains a well. It is, however, round, and therefore probably not Roman, though it may have been used by them. After leaving this the track crosses the later Portway from Sarum to Silchester, and proceeds by King John's Hill to Great Litchfield[2] Down, where is a large round camp at Burghclere. Adjoining it is a smaller square Roman camp, and this is probably that of which Dr. Gibson[3] speaks as Roman, and containing building. On Beacon Hill, a little above this, near High Clere, is a British camp and hut dwellings. The road then follows a well-defined ridge, and passes through the centre of a large camp at Wallbury. Near Bedwyn, before reaching Marlborough, is another large camp at Chisbury; and further south another at Fosbury.

It must be remembered that the Bericus, whom I have already mentioned as inciting the invasion, was of the race of Commius, King of the Attrebates, who had their settlements in the north of Hampshire and Berkshire. It is likely, therefore, that he would have brought his allies along the route familiar to him, and if he had already arranged for support to his cause, it would still further explain the march. There is, indeed, some reason for supposing that he had been expelled from his kingdom by Cunobelinus, King of the Catuvellauni, whose sons Plautius encountered in battle. As the Romans made peace with the Dobuni, who had been subject to the Catuvellauni, it is possible that they found a population ready to welcome them as deliverers; this they would be the more ready to do, as the Dobuni were of a different stock and retain their distinctive features to this day.

It is, I think, strongly confirmatory of my supposition that the Roman march was along this line of country, that among the coins[4] found at Farley Heath and elsewhere in the neighbourhood, are several of Bericus or Vericus, son of Commius. Commius was the King of the Attrebates of Gaul, who was the guide and friend of Cæsar on his invasion, and afterwards fled from him into Britain. There must therefore have intervened a second Commius or Bericus between the time of Cæsar and Claudius.

[1] Probably from St. Rock, patron saint of pilgrims. Compare St. Rock's Hill, Chichester.
[2] There are many Litchfields near camps in Hants. They doubtless commemorate Saxon battles.   [3] Gibson's Camden.
[4] 'Surrey Archæol. Soc. Trans.,' vols. i. and ii.

That Wallingford was the accepted place for passing the Thames we know from the fact that the Conqueror crossed there, and that Cuthwulf, of the West Saxons, had also probably passed at the same place.[1]

The advance of so large an army as this into a hostile country can hardly have failed to leave some marks of its progress, especially as it is not likely that the General would cut himself off from his base. On the contrary, there is little doubt but that all along the road he would establish posts. We are told that he had great difficulty in finding the enemy, and had to seek them out in their defences.

No doubt such fortresses of the enemy as were stormed, and lay along the road, were utilized as posts, and where others were constructed one would not expect to find them as large and perfect as were made when the occupation of the country was assured.

Now, both Farley Heath and Hillborough lie close to this track. They are of a somewhat irregular square, such as we may suppose to have been hastily thrown up. Neither the position nor the defences of either are such as would be likely to be chosen deliberately for the purposes of permanent warfare, though they would very well answer a temporary purpose. The distance between them—from ten to twelve miles—is, perhaps, as much as an army would safely accomplish on an unknown road with the river Wey to cross.

A stage beyond Hillborough is Jockey's Ring, Cæsar's Camp, or Tuksbury, as it is variously called. This is a large irregular early camp, but Bishop Pococke[2] says that there was on Brigborough a square Roman camp. The six-inch Ordnance map shows Bricksbury, which seems identical with Tuksbury; but north of this, a small square camp is shown on the Ordnance and on my map. This is doubtless a Roman work, and from its size intended for a fortified post rather than a permanent camp.

In the other direction the next stage would be at Dorking, where a camp is supposed to have been at Bury Hill. Adjoining to this is the Nore, which, as I have already pointed out, is an accompaniment of a Roman camp.

Some way south of Reigate is a very curious place called Thundersfield Castle. The late Mr. Godwin-Austen thought this was such a British camp as described by Cæsar. Certainly it answers to the description, but it has to my eyes too regular a look for such a date. It rather suggests the work of the West Saxon kings, and it was doubtless the Thundersfield where so many Witenagemots were held, and which Kemble could not identify. The name, however, seems to betoken an early origin. In any case it, perhaps, lies too far out of the line to be much concerned in this march.

After the success of the campaign, these camps would for some time remain as stations, and afterwards decline, as Hillborough seems to have done, or grow into

---

[1] Green, 'Making of England,' p. 123.   [2] Page 162.

towns, as Farley Heath.   After a very short time the Roman road was taken through Rochester to London, and this route lost its importance for ever, as a magnificent new road, much on the lines of the present, was constructed leading directly to the West of England.

The account of the campaign is so slight that we have no means of judging if it were a rapid march or a slowly progressive fight.

Plautius landed in the spring of A.D. 43,[1] and reached the neighbourhood of London.   There he halted, and sent for the Emperor Claudius to come and complete the conquest.   Claudius was six months going and returning to Rome, where he celebrated his triumph in A.D. 44.   He only stayed sixteen days altogether in the island.   Dion states that Plautius sent for Claudius on account of the doubtful nature of his position, and that he employed the time in securing his conquests. That he had done this effectually is clear, since Claudius travelled straight to the Thames, crossed it, and joined the army, and marched on and took Camulodunum.[2] It seems evident that the courtly Plautius simply reserved the crowning victory for his imperial master.

One of the principal lieutenants of Plautius was the Vespasian afterwards emperor, and we read in Suetonius[3] that Vespasian 'Inde in Britanniam translatus tricies cum hoste conflixit Duas validissimas gentes superque viginti oppida et insulam Vectem Britanniæ proximam in ditionem redegit partim Auli Plautii legati consularis partim Claudii ipsius ductu.'   If the statement of Suetonius can be taken as accurate, we must assume that, probably while Plautius was watching the enemy on the other side of the Thames, Vespasian was occupied in subduing this part of the South of England.   Here, as stated above, he fought thirty battles, and reduced to subjection two very powerful peoples, and over twenty fortified places, and the Isle of Wight.

It is evident that we must expect to find traces of what must have been no inconsiderable struggle.   The whole of it may have extended over some years, although begun at the period mentioned; this is indeed confirmed by the story of Suetonius, that in A.D. 47 Vespasian, being in the greatest danger during a battle, was rescued by the desperate bravery of his son Titus.   It was in A.D. 47 that Plautius celebrated his triumph at Rome.   If we consider that Vespasian assisted in forcing the passage of the Thames, even if he did not accompany his leader further, we shall be led to suppose that the scene of his campaign was probably on the Wiltshire side of the Isle of Wight.   He would naturally first attack the enemy from the neighbourhood of his allies the Dobuni, so as to secure a base of supply, and also to protect them from their foes.

[1] Dr. Guest.   [2] Colchester or Maldon.   [3] Lib. xc. 4.

This part and Hampshire were the seats of the most advanced Belgic tribes, who had been under the dominion of Divitiacus the Gaulish king, and Stonehenge was their sacred centre.[1] The large camp near Ambresbury is known as Vespasian's Camp, but probably has as little claim to the title as the numerous Cæsar's camps have to theirs. In Wiltshire and Hampshire are a good many more than the twenty oppida that Vespasian is said to have taken; but, as I have no local knowledge, I say nothing of them.

The Belgæ, who were evidently the leading nationality, being conquered in their own headquarters, and the harbours of Southampton and Portsmouth secured, it is likely that the remainder of the country could be brought to subjection without great trouble. We know, indeed, that the Romans made peace with Cogidubnos, whom they established as King of the Regni, who inhabited the coast of Sussex.

In A.D. 120 Ptolemy describes Portsmouth as a 'great harbour,' and doubtless some station would be established here by Vespasian, even if Porchester Castle, whose Roman walls still remain, were of later date.

A station and harbour being established, the next thing would be to connect it with a road; and as soon as the Romans became at all settled, they would not be content with the native trackways, but would carry out their own straight and magnificent roads.

London quickly became an important Roman town and port, and it is somewhat remarkable that a straight line drawn between it and Porchester passes exactly along the road I have already mentioned as passing by Castle Copse on Blackdown, along High Street Green, by Hascombe Camp to the town at Farley Heath. Both Blackdown and Hascombe Hill are famous for the extent of land they cover as look-out places, and have been used as semaphore stations.

I have not been able to explore the country between Porchester and Blackdown, but I note on the Ordnance map a Castle Farm at West Harting Down on the exact line, and on a line to Havant is Rowland's[2] Castle, where Roman remains have been found. There are no signs of a road on the map, but the road through the Hartings might be on the track.

It is possible, however, that the direction of the road is an accident only, and that it was merely a branch from the Chichester road of which I have spoken; but it is remarkable that from Farley this line would exactly pick up the straight road from Letherhead to London. There are some evidences of a Roman road here, at Ashtead and again at Ewell. The course of the Stane Street near Epsom is not

---

[1] Pliny states that Druidism was suppressed in Britain in the time of Claudius.

[2] Probably equivalent to Rough-lands, or, as some think, to Road-lands; it has nothing to do with Roland.

very clear, and if this road by Ewell existed before the Stane Street, it is possible this latter was taken into it somewhere at this part. My conclusion is that these camps and this road date from the conquests of Vespasian, or at a time soon after.

At a date a little later still, probably under the enlightened rule of Agricola, the more important and carefully constructed Stane Street was built, and became the highway to Chichester, and the Portsmouth traffic was possibly taken into it after passing through Havant. Such camps as those of Hascombe would not long be required for military purposes, and probably enjoyed but a short career. The road this way, never probably very well constructed, and traversing in great part a clayey country, may have become disused, and survived only in such parts as High Street, that lay along a ridge.

However, this road must have been still in existence when the Roman villa at Chiddingfold was flourishing, and that was most probably of late date.

When the town of Petersfield was made, the Portsmouth road came through there and passed, as now, through Godalming and Guildford. This route is evidently a more suitable one for commercial purposes. On this there are two places called Causeway, which seems to argue a Roman origin.

On Walton Downs, which may be taken as the extreme north of the ridgeway, are shown on the six-inch Ordnance map, three square camps of varying size; the smaller has very much the same appearance as those at Burghclere and Aldershot. The latter scales about 200 feet by 175 feet inside. It could therefore only have served for a fort; but it has a double vallum and foss. The small size is such as we should expect Plautius to form on the road, since he could obviously not afford to leave a large detachment in each.

It is exceptional for a Roman camp to be on a high hill, and that makes it still more probable that Hascombe was an early work, at a time when an extended look-out was essential.

Adjoining Cæsar's Camp is Tweseldown Hill. Some controversy has lately gone on as to the meaning of this prefix.[1] Charters 596, 633, 786, which apply the word to an oak, a tree, and a way, leave little doubt but that Dr. Isaac Taylor's explanation, 'forked,' is correct.

With regard to the Leatherhead road, it is to be noted that the six-inch Ordnance shows, at Pachesham, about a mile N.W. of the town, a square camp called the Mounts, where Roman tiles and brass coins were found in 1859. There are also recorded at Ashtead several finds of Roman remains.

[1] *Notes and Queries*, 1889.

CHAPTER XIII.

THE SAXON OCCUPATION.

OF the early Saxon history of the county we have little information, and that little is chiefly concerned with its northern part. As I have already pointed out, it is likely that the greater part of the county remained in an unsettled state. It must be remembered that, besides the Weald proper and the swampy valleys of the Wey and the Mole, a great part of Surrey was in almost a forest condition.

The Forest of Windsor covered the north-east corner, and Richard I. afforested the whole of this part of the county; that is to say, he brought it all under the strict and oppressive forest law. It may be doubtful, however, if this law was ever strictly enforced in this district, since there were constant protests from the people of Guildford and others.

In the time of Henry III., the rights claimed by the king were relinquished, and the forest restricted to its former limits. As I have before stated, the term 'forest' does not necessarily imply dense trees, but merely rough and wild ground excluded from the ordinary jurisdiction; there is no reason to suppose, for instance, that the desolate heaths of Bagshot and Chobham were ever wooded.

Till a late time there were also parks at Guildford, Witley, Godalming, Hascombe, and Farnham, and these parks were wild places set apart for hunting.

The kingdom of Wessex sought no extension on this side; it had enough to do to conquer the West of England, where rich and prosperous cities held out more tempting promise of spoil.

The dedication to Saxon gods of the hills and places on this wild, heathy, eastern border of Wessex seems to point to it as the mark or boundary land at an early period. Instances of such names are Wanborough (Wodenborough), Thursley, Tewsley, Polsted, Paulshot, Drake Hill, and perhaps Rodborough.[1] To this group belongs also Peperharow, on the name of which, hitherto doubtful, I can throw some

[1] Rev. G. F. Davies.

light. The latter part of the word certainly means 'a heathen temple, or perhaps the grove without the temple.'[1] A similar affix is found over the border at Basing, called in Charter No. 72 of A.D. 688, 'Besinga hearh.' It has been suggested that the prefix 'Peper' came from the Norman family of Pipard, but that would involve too great an anachronism to be possible. Charter 145, Cart. Sax.,[2] of about the date A.D. 725, contains a grant from Nunna, King of the South Saxons, of land for founding an oratory 'in loco qui appellatur Piperinges juxta flumen Tarente id est IIII tributarios.' This place was undoubtedly Peppering[3] on the river Arun. The charter is valuable as identifying the Arun with the Tarent, which again has been identified by Mr. Henry Bradley with the Trisanton of Ptolemy. I pointed out in the *Academy* some years ago this identification of the Arun and the Tarent; it had also been previously conjectured by Mr. Napper. The only authority I could give was Dallaway,[4] who, however, does not give his reference. This charter completes the identification as to which there has been constant question. The name Pipers occurs also in Sussex at Piper's Bridge, near Northchapel, where there is a round camp, as I believe, undescribed. There is also a Pipers near Elsted, in Sussex, of which I shall speak further on. The name occurs in Gloucestershire, and, I fancy, will be found common in England. There is a Piper's Hill close to Hambledon in Hampshire, and another at Sarson, further west in the county.

Aubrey mentions a great wide trench and bank as existing on Worplesdon Common, running from south-east to north-west, and having the bank on the west side. This may have been connected with a similar bank that crosses the road at Charles Hill on the other side of the Hogsback, and this may have been the boundary line of the West Saxon kingdom, and perhaps Charles stands for Ceawlin.

It was probably not till the conquest of these parts by Wulfhere of Mercia, in 661, that settled government and civilization began again. At the same time, Wulfhere conquered Sussex, and the Jutish kingdom of the Meonwaras, and the Isle of Wight; these latter he handed over to his convert, the dependent King of the South Saxons, but certainly Surrey, and possibly the Weald, remained under the powerful and enlightened Mercian rule for the next 160 years—a long period, the meaning of which should be kept in mind.

It is said that Eadwine of Northumbria had previously subdued all England except Kent, but this expression is too vague to include the Weald and the land of the South Saxons without further evidence. Professor Green's[5] map of this period should be taken with reservations. The same remark applies to Kent and the Weald.

---

[1] Grimm, 'Deutsche Mytho.,' p. 59, cited by W. H. Stevenson in the *Academy*, March 17, 1888, p. 189.   [2] Kemble, lxxv.

[3] Piperinge, *temp.* Hen. IV.   [4] 'History of Sussex,' I. cliii.   [5] 'Making of England.'

The author of the article (before referred to) in the *Saturday Review* was, as far as I know, the first to bring out the full significance to the history of Surrey of this fact of Mercian supremacy. All the studies I have made since go to confirm the suggestion that the Saxon settlement of the country dates from this period. A significant fact is that nearly the whole of this territory seems to have passed into the personal, as distinguished from the official, possession of the Kings of Mercia; there it remained until it passed over to their successors, the Kings of Wessex, and was disposed of by the will of King Alfred.

That this part of Surrey was a border country, to which particular attention was paid both by the Mercian and West Saxon kings, we have evidence in the creation or adoption of the 'castles' at Ockley, and afterwards at Thundersfield, in both of which so many Witenagemots were held.

In 660, Wulfhere of Mercia had created a Sub-regulus of Surrey, and we have a charter (No. 39), purporting to be of 675, by Frithenwald Sub-regulus, granting to the newly-founded Abbey of Chertsey very extensive possessions in Surrey; this includes land at Bookham and Effingham, Clandon, Albury, Compton, and Henley. Kemble marks the charter as doubtful, and it was possibly reconstructed, if not fabricated for the purpose of confirmation by Offa[1] in 787.

I have already stated that in 661 the Mercians handed over the Isle of Wight and the land of the Meonwaras to the South Saxons. This miserable people could not, however, long keep the gift, since, in 686, Ceadwalla of Wessex takes the Isle of Wight, and evidently the land of the Jutes at the same time. What is more curious is that he is found in the same and the next year harrying Kent. To get to Kent he must either have made his way through the South Saxon kingdom, or have crossed Mercian territory from Farnham along the Hogsback—it seems certain the Mercians would not have allowed him to cross nearer London. It is perhaps most likely that he went through Sussex.

In 688 Ceadwalla signs at Basing the charter (No. 145) that I have already referred to, by which he gives to the Abbey of Winchester lands at Farnham, Bentley, Chert, Cusanweoh (? Cowshot), and some other places.

From 764 to 791 we have grants[2] of lands at Henfield, Petworth, and other places in the Weald of Sussex; these are always described as 'sylvaticæ terræ,' and are always confirmed by 'domino meo' Offa. It seems certain that it was only under the firm rule of the Mercian kings that the South Saxons advanced into the Weald. A good deal of speculation has been bestowed on the date and reason of formation of the divisions of Rapes peculiar to this county.

I find it difficult to believe that such divisions could have survived the anarchy

---

[1] Cart. Sax., No. 251.   [2] Nos. 197, 206, 262.

of three centuries, and, judging also from the unusually formal lines of the boundaries, I incline to think that they probably date from this period, and were the creation of Mercian rule.   There seem always, at this time, to have been several kings or dukes at the same time in Sussex, and the people of Hastings and Pevensey are spoken of as warring with King Offa quite independently of the South Saxons.

Probably the numerous places ending in 'fold' in this division date from this period, especially as Kingsfold seems to point to the time that the kings held Ockley.

In Charter No. 258, of A.D. 790, Beorhtric of Wessex, son-in-law to Offa of Mercia, obtains lands at Meon in exchange with Hamele, 'fidellisimo principi meo ;' the charter also recites that King Kenwulf had previously confirmed these lands to Hamele, and received 'precium in auro purissimo.'

In 823 Ecgberht of Wessex conquers Surrey, and in the next year at a synod at Ockley grants by charter (No. 377) land about the river Meon to 'Wlfheardo prefecto meo.'

It will be evident to everyone who has studied local names that there is a very great resemblance between the place-names of this south-west corner of Surrey and the adjoining parts of Sussex and Hampshire.   It may, in fact, almost be called a duplication, and can hardly be sufficiently accounted for by accident.   I am inclined to think that it was from this Jutish kingdom, about the Meons, that this part of Surrey was settled, and most likely in Saxon times.

I am of those who find it impossible to believe that there was any total destruction of the old life and population, although with the destruction of the aristocracy civilization was certainly for a time annihilated, or driven into the large cities, whence after a time it again emerged triumphant though sadly injured.

It is unlikely, however, that even in the Roman time there was any great opulence or importance in this part, which was to such a great extent moor or forest.

That the Saxons could of themselves contribute anything to civilization is, I think, sufficiently disproved by the miserable condition into which the South Saxons fell.   These Saxons probably did, as records of the sack of Anderida tell, exterminate the older inhabitants, and being then cut off by their position from intercourse with Romano-British culture, they fell into that state of gross barbarism in which Wilfrid of Ripon found them.   I make allowance for some ecclesiastical exaggeration in the account, but as late as A.D. 686 the Isle of Wight was an independent pagan kingdom.

Though I do not believe that the inhabitants of this part were in any way exterminated, yet there must have been plenty of land open to settlers, and it is probable that the new governors would be anxious to introduce sub-lords whom they could make responsible.

It seems likely from the charters I have cited above that the Jutish settlers of the Meons were dispossessed of their holdings, which were in a position inconveniently near to Winchester, which became the capital of the kingdom. The shores of Southampton Water, and probably Portsmouth, would also be likely to be the first to be taken away from them.

I suppose, then, that they were pushed up into the corner of Surrey, very likely travelling along the Roman road that I have conjectured existed.

On this road, in the north-west corner of Sussex, lies the village of Elsted. This is too common a name to found any argument upon, but it is remarkable that adjoining Elsted in Sussex are a chain of barrows called the Devil's Jumps. Close to Elstead in Surrey are the well-known Devil's Jumps adjoining Hindhead. These appear to be natural hills that accidentally stand detached. On the other side of the Surrey Elstead there are, however, a chain of barrows very similar to those in Sussex, and I think it is quite possible that the name may have at some time got transferred from them to the other natural hills. These latter barrows were explored by the Rev. C. F. Kerry, but nothing was found. I have before mentioned that there is a Pipers adjoining Elsted in Sussex, and Peperharow adjoins Elstead in Surrey.

In the heart of the country of the Meonwaras in Hampshire is Hambledon, famous as the birthplace of cricket. This is a name that occurs perpetually throughout England. It is supposed to be derived from a Celtic word which means water. Close to this particular Hambledon is the river Hamble that runs into Southampton Water. The intrusion of a 'b' or a 'p' is a frequent phonetic change; thus the Kemele in Wiltshire of the charters[1] has become Kemble, and Hamtun become Hampton. A place here called Hamele-en-le-Rhys has been derived from the personal name Hamele. On page 128 I have mentioned Hamele, fidelissimus princeps of Beorhtric of Wessex, as a landowner in these parts. In 'Archæologia'[2] this place is derived from the personal name, a name also recorded as of a man of distinction in Worcestershire.[3]

It is hardly, however, open to doubt, seeing the frequency with which the place name Hamelandun occurs in the charters, but that it comes from the older root; this is the more certain as the name doubtless corresponds with the words Emly, and Amele,[4] which were old names of the Mole, and frequent river-names. The former gave the name to the Hundred of Emlybridge.

It is worth consideration, however, whether the personal name may not have

[1] No. 63. [2] Vol. l., p. 251. [3] Charter No. 256. [4] Sur. Arch. Trans., Vol. V., p. 18.

17

arisen from the possession, as became the rule in later times.   There are several instances in the charters that make one suspect that such may sometimes, even at so early a date, have been the case.

Adjoining this Hampshire Hambledon is the down on which is the large camp known as Old Winchester, and near it is Beacon Hill.   Close to this the six-inch Ordnance map gives Chidden Down, Chidden Holt, Chidden (hamlet), Chidden Farm, Highden Wood, Highden Farm, and Heydown Barn.

In the remarkable series of Winchester charters relating to Hampshire, we have one, No. 976, of the year A.D. 956, granting land in 'Cittandene.'   Among the boundaries are 'hamelandunæ hyrth' and 'citwara becon.'   In No. 982 of the same year, relating to land at Meon, we have also mention of 'citwara becon.'   I may add here that many of the boundaries are easily to be identified by the six-inch Ordnance map.

Now, in Surrey we have Hambledon, which, however, has nothing like a river, or even a stream, although there are springs.   Adjoining it is Chiddingfold, Hyden's Ball and Heath, and Hyde Stile.   With regard to the name Hyden, the form Highdown, or Highden, seems to be a modern gloss.   The word occurs commonly throughout England in various forms, and though there are some entries of 'hig dun' in the charters, the usual form is 'heidene.'   There would be as much reason to turn Hyde Park into Highdown Park.   I take no account of the duplication of such a name as Witley.   'Chidding' is, however, by no means a common prefix. Chiddingstone, in Kent, also a Jutish kingdom, and Chiddingly,[1] in Sussex, are the best known instances.

If, as I suppose, the dispossessed Jutes moved up the line of the old Roman road, it is not unlikely that, settling in the new country, they should repeat the names of the places they came from.   I am also certainly inclined to attribute to survivors of this tribe of 'citwaras' the name of Chitty, one of the most common in West Sussex and Surrey.   Pipers, Lythe and Rake appear on the line in Hampshire, Sussex, and Surrey; and near Petersfield is Ciddy Hall.   The large camp I have spoken of as called Old Winchester has often been alluded to as the headquarters of the Meonwaras.   They may have occupied it, though that would be an unusual thing for Saxons to do, except in war; but it is evident that it is old British, and was Caer-Gwent before the new Caer-Gwent, now Winchester, was created.

Among the boundaries in Charters No. 982, relating to Meon, and No. 674 and 787, relating to Clere, in Hampshire, a name occurs which promises to be of some interest.   This is in the first, 'punches hyl,' and again 'pungches hyl,' and in the second and third 'pungchesdune and 'pungesdone.'   Mr. Birch, the editor, has

---

[1] Citangaleahge, Charter 764.

spelt these in the text as 'wunches,' but in a note has stated that it is doubtful if the first letter is a 'w' or a 'p.' The Saxon 'w,' it must be noted, is very like a 'p.' I have no doubt it must be a 'p.' The only local name I can find on the six-inch Ordnance map that answers to these is 'Punsholt Farm' and 'Punsholt Lane,' near West Meon, and these are in the right position.

I had always regarded the Devil's Punchbowl, near Hindhead, as a fancy name, but I have little doubt now but that it is connected with these names, though the 'bowl' part is doubtless an addition, caused by false analogy. Punchestown, near Dublin, has also, I believe, been taken to be a modern form, but may really be a survival. I do not think this use of the word 'Punch,' as a place-name, has been previously recorded. I am under a strong impression that I have noted it on modern maps elsewhere, but I cannot verify this.

I do not find any word approaching this in Gaelic, Irish, or Cornish dictionaries that I have consulted ; but in the old Franco-Breton Dictionary, by Rostrenen, I find 'Puncgz' interpreted as a well or cistern. This looks like a probable root, and the hills may have had their name from some artificial supply of water for cattle ; perhaps from Roman works of the sort of which there seem to be some at Burgh Clere, which is probably part of the Clere alluded to in the charter. There is also, near Meon, a camp marked Roman, apparently very like Hillborough and Farley ; it stands on a ridgeway.

What I have given are only samples of the common duplication of names ; I find it difficult to believe that they are accidental. There is, indeed, nothing that is not what we should expect, and though I wish to guard myself most carefully from laying undue stress on such coincidences, I certainly think a careful study of them may, after due sifting, lead to interesting results.

GENERAL INDEX.

Lightning Source UK Ltd.
Milton Keynes UK
UKOW020636071012

200184UK00007B/82/P